CHRIS
ROCK

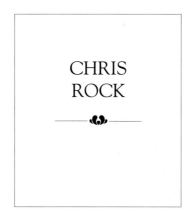

CHRIS ROCK

Rose Blue and

Corinne J. Naden

CHELSEA HOUSE PUBLISHERS
Philadelphia

Chelsea House Publishers

Editor in Chief	Stephen Reginald
Production Manager	Pamela Loos
Director of Photography	Judy L. Hasday
Art Director	Sara Davis
Managing Editor	James D. Gallagher
Senior Production Editor	LeeAnne Gelletly

Staff for CHRIS ROCK

Project Editor	James D. Gallagher
Associate Art Director	Takeshi Takahashi
Designer	21st Century Publishing and Communications
Cover Designer	Keith Trego
Cover photos	AP Photo/HBO, David Lee

The Chelsea House World Wide Web address is
http://www.chelseahouse.com

3 5 7 9 8 6 4 2

Library of Congress Cataloging-in-Publication Data

Blue, Rose.
Chris Rock, comedian / Rose Blue and Corinne J. Naden
    p.   cm. —(Black Americans of Achievement)
Includes bibliographical references and index.
Summary: A biography of the popular comedian, known for his stand-up routines and for his role on the late-night television program, "Saturday Night Live."
ISBN 0-7910-5277-X (hc.). — ISBN 0-7910-5278-8 (pb.)
1. Rock, Chris —Juvenile literature. 2. Comedians—United States—Biography —Juvenile literature. 3. Afro-American comedians—United States—Biography —Juvenile literature. [1. Rock, Chris. 2. Comedians. 3. Afro-Americans— Biography.] I. Naden, Corinne J. II. Title. III. Series.
PN2287.R717B59   1999
792.7'028'092—dc21
[B]   99–39931
                                                                             CIP

Frontis: A "stand-up" guy, comedian Chris Rock has hit the big time with his off-beat style, attracting audiences of all ethnic backgrounds and all ages.

CONTENTS

BLACK AMERICANS OF ACHIEVEMENT

HENRY AARON
baseball great

KAREEM ABDUL-JABBAR
basketball great

MUHAMMAD ALI
heavyweight champion

RICHARD ALLEN
religious leader and social activist

MAYA ANGELOU
author

LOUIS ARMSTRONG
musician

ARTHUR ASHE
tennis great

JOSEPHINE BAKER
entertainer

JAMES BALDWIN
author

TYRA BANKS
model

BENJAMIN BANNEKER
scientist and mathematician

COUNT BASIE
bandleader and composer

ANGELA BASSETT
actress

ROMARE BEARDEN
artist

HALLE BERRY
actress

MARY MCLEOD BETHUNE
educator

GEORGE WASHINGTON CARVER
botanist

JOHNNIE COCHRAN
lawyer

SEAN "PUFFY" COMBS
music producer

BILL COSBY
entertainer

MILES DAVIS
musician

FREDERICK DOUGLASS
abolitionist editor

CHARLES DREW
physician

W. E. B. DU BOIS
scholar and activist

PAUL LAURENCE DUNBAR
poet

DUKE ELLINGTON
bandleader and composer

RALPH ELLISON
author

JULIUS ERVING
basketball great

LOUIS FARRAKHAN
political activist

ELLA FITZGERALD
singer

ARETHA FRANKLIN
entertainer

MORGAN FREEMAN
actor

MARCUS GARVEY
black nationalist leader

JOSH GIBSON
baseball great

WHOOPI GOLDBERG
entertainer

CUBA GOODING JR.
actor

ALEX HALEY
author

PRINCE HALL
social reformer

JIMI HENDRIX
musician

MATTHEW HENSON
explorer

GREGORY HINES
performer

BILLIE HOLIDAY
singer

LENA HORNE
entertainer

WHITNEY HOUSTON
singer and actress

LANGSTON HUGHES
poet

JANET JACKSON
musician

JESSE JACKSON
civil-rights leader and politician

MICHAEL JACKSON
entertainer

SAMUEL L. JACKSON *actor*	JOE LOUIS *heavyweight champion*	ROSA PARKS *civil-rights leader*	TINA TURNER *entertainer*
T. D. JAKES *religious leader*	RONALD MCNAIR *astronaut*	COLIN POWELL *military leader*	ALICE WALKER *author*
JACK JOHNSON *heavyweight champion*	MALCOLM X *militant black leader*	PAUL ROBESON *singer and actor*	MADAM C. J. WALKER *entrepreneur*
MAGIC JOHNSON *basketball great*	BOB MARLEY *musician*	JACKIE ROBINSON *baseball great*	BOOKER T. WASHINGTON *educator*
SCOTT JOPLIN *composer*	THURGOOD MARSHALL *Supreme Court justice*	CHRIS ROCK *comedian and actor*	DENZEL WASHINGTON *actor*
BARBARA JORDAN *politician*	TERRY MCMILLAN *author*	DIANA ROSS *entertainer*	J. C. WATTS *politician*
MICHAEL JORDAN *basketball great*	TONI MORRISON *author*	WILL SMITH *actor*	VANESSA WILLIAMS *singer and actress*
CORETTA SCOTT KING *civil-rights leader*	ELIJAH MUHAMMAD *religious leader*	WESLEY SNIPES *actor*	OPRAH WINFREY *entertainer*
MARTIN LUTHER KING, JR. *civil-rights leader*	EDDIE MURPHY *entertainer*	CLARENCE THOMAS *Supreme Court justice*	TIGER WOODS *golf star*
LEWIS LATIMER *scientist*	JESSE OWENS *champion athlete*	SOJOURNER TRUTH *antislavery activist*	RICHARD WRIGHT *author*
SPIKE LEE *filmmaker*	SATCHEL PAIGE *baseball great*	HARRIET TUBMAN *antislavery activist*	
CARL LEWIS *champion athlete*	CHARLIE PARKER *musician*	NAT TURNER *slave revolt leader*	

ON
ACHIEVEMENT

Coretta Scott King

Bᴇꜰᴏʀᴇ ʏᴏᴜ ʙᴇɢɪɴ this book, I hope you will ask yourself what the word *excellence* means to you. I think it's a question we should all ask, and keep asking as we grow older and change. Because the truest answer to it should never change. When you think of excellence, perhaps you think of success at work; or of becoming wealthy; or meeting the right person, getting married, and having a good family life.

Those goals are worth striving for, but there is a better way to look at excellence. As Martin Luther King Jr. said in one of his last sermons, "I want you to be first in love. I want you to be first in moral excellence. I want you to be first in generosity. If you want to be important, wonderful. If you want to be great, wonderful. But recognize that he who is greatest among you shall be your servant."

My husband knew that the true meaning of achievement is service. When I met him, in 1952, he was already ordained as a Baptist minister and was working toward a doctoral degree at Boston University. I was studying at the New England Conservatory and dreamed of accomplishments in music. We married a year later, and after I graduated the following year we moved to Montgomery, Alabama. We didn't know it then, but our notions of achievement were about to undergo a dramatic change.

You may have read or heard about what happened next. What began with the boycott of a local bus line grew into a national crusade, and by the time he was assassinated in 1968 my husband had fashioned a black movement powerful enough to shatter forever the practice of racial segregation. What you may not have read about is where he learned to resist injustice without compromising his religious beliefs.

He adopted a strategy of nonviolence from a man of a different race, who lived in a different country and even practiced a different religion. The man was Mahatma Gandhi, the great leader of India, who devoted his life to serving humanity in the spirit of love and nonviolence. It was in these principles that Martin discovered his method for social reform. More than anything else, those two principles were the key to his achievements.

These books are about African Americans who served society through the excellence of their achievements. They form part of the rich history of black men and women in America—a history of stunning accomplishments in every field of human endeavor, from literature and art to science, industry, education, diplomacy, athletics, jurisprudence, even polar exploration.

Not all of the people in this history had the same ideals, but I think you will find that all of them had something in common. Like Martin Luther King Jr., they all decided to become "drum majors" and serve humanity. In that principle—whether it was expressed in books, inventions, or song— they found a goal and a guide outside themselves that showed them a way to serve others instead of living only for themselves.

Reading the stories of these courageous men and women not only helps us discover the principles that we will use to guide our own lives; it also teaches us about our black heritage and about America itself. It is crucial for us to know the heroes and heroines of our history and to realize that the price we paid in our struggle for equality in America was dear. But we must also understand that we have gotten as far as we have partly because America's democratic system and ideals made it possible.

We are still struggling with racism and prejudice. But the great men and women in this series are a tribute to the spirit of the country in which they have flourished. And that makes their stories special and worth knowing.

1

ENTER LAUGHING

❧

"I'M WATCHING THE news. Like, Tupac Shakur was assassinated! Biggie Smalls was assassinated! Struck down by assassin's bullets. Assassinated?" The speaker then shouts at his audience: "No, no, no. . . . Martin Luther King was *assassinated*. Malcolm X was *assassinated*. JFK was *assassinated*. Them two niggas got *shot*!"

The first timers in the audience at the comedy club gasp audibly. They glance at one another, their eyes questioning, "Did I hear right? Is that what that man said?" "That man," to whom they are referring, is standing on the stage sort of smiling and staring out at the crowd. His eyes widen a bit, and he pauses, waiting for the laugh that comes as if on cue.

The man who elicited gasps and then laughs is Chris Rock, comedian, who has just delivered his comments on gangster rap. This skinny, 33-year-old with his stylish goatee and raspy voice gathers his material from contemporary society, often outrageously commenting on race, ethnicity, drugs, violence, women, and people he feels deserve his barbs. Chris Rock has put it all together and created his own unique style of delivery. He shocks. He disturbs. And he makes people laugh.

That evening, as on many others, Chris performs as comics have done before him and will do after him. He has learned the essence of his material. He

Audiences who know Chris Rock's style are not fooled by his boyish face and broad grin. Loud and forthright, his comedy routines shock, provoke, and often offend, but they make people laugh and sometimes think, which is what Chris wants.

knows the history of humor. He draws on the truth of tough, tragic times for African Americans. He knows how the past and the present relate to his art. Above all, Chris knows the truth of the old saying "Laughter is the best medicine."

Of course, ethnic humor is not new. People have been laughing at themselves, poking fun at their suffering because of race, religion, or gender for about as long as anyone can remember. Comic greats such as Eddie Cantor and Henny Youngman drew upon the experiences of Jews—their people—in their humor. If it seemed that the anguish of anti-Semitism left no room for merriment, Jewish comics could draw a smile and a laugh, making the world a bit more livable.

Other comics have done the same. Margo Gomez, a Latina, is a funny lady on the rise as she takes on a double-barreled reason—ethnicity and gender—to keep from crying. Superstar Whoopi Goldberg, one of the best-known, most popular, and most durable of comedians, is still drawing laughs by poking fun at people's prejudices. She joins a battery of African-American comedy stars whose ranks include Bill Cosby, Flip Wilson, Richard Pryor, Eddie Murphy, Redd Foxx, and a host of others.

Chris admires Goldberg, even though his routines often include what some, and certainly many women, regard as his disparaging attitude toward the opposite sex and monologues about their inadequacies. He often makes a great point in his routines of saying that women just cannot keep quiet. Chris makes an exception of Goldberg as well as white comedian Ellen DeGeneres. He also respects what Bill Cosby has accomplished in show business.

"I've always loved Cosby," he says. Rock believes that more than any other comedian, Cosby has managed to figure out how to be funny at different stages of his life and his career. When Cosby was in his early 20s and starting out, his humor was different

Flip Wilson was television's first successful African-American variety-show host, and he was a master at getting laughs from ethnic humor. His sketches included himself, bewigged and costumed, as the wisecracking, brassy ghetto queen Geraldine Jones, who introduced the memorable phrase "The devil made me do it."

from the style he adopted when he became a husband and father on his highly popular and enduring *The Cosby Show*. Cosby's style changed yet again after his children grew up and moved out of the house. Chris still respects Cosby despite the fact that the older comedian has so far declined to appear on Chris's television show and has criticized the young comedian for his language.

Many people say that great comedians, whatever their ethnicity, share common experiences of pain, which for some becomes a large part of their style. Lenny Bruce, who has been called the angriest of the '60s comedians, was persecuted for his satiric routines in which he used obscene language. In 1964, he was convicted on pornography charges and banned from performing in New York City's nightclubs. Richard Pryor is the son of a prostitute, and he has suffered from multiple sclerosis and periods of severe depression. Martin Lawrence, star of *Martin*, suffered a severe mental breakdown, was charged with gun possession, and was banned from the NBC television network after he used profanity on the late-night show *Saturday Night Live*.

As a teen, Chris learned quickly about the pain of racism. He was sent to a white school where, he has said, there were about 10 black youngsters among some 2,000 white students, and racism was rampant. Chris suffered taunts and ethnic slurs and beatings, and although it was the 1970s, he recalls that for him it was like the 1940s.

Chris did hate the school and his experiences there, but he has not created all of his comedy style from his background. He is an avid admirer of another comedian whom he emulates—the late Sam Kinison. Kinison was a white comedian who was killed in a car accident in 1992. Shamelessly irreverent, he was best known for his 1991 TV show *The Brave New World of Charlie Hoover* and for his stint on *Saturday Night Live*. Often compared to Richard Pryor for "dangerous raging on stage and off," Kinison was also famous for equaling Lenny Bruce in bad taste and controversial comedy. If he sometimes sounded like a preacher shouting his material from the pulpit, it might have been because both his parents were preachers.

Chris, himself the grandson of a preacher, incorporates parts of Kinison's style into his own. He says that he loved Sam because he was so completely honest. Calling Kinison the "white Richard Pryor," Chris gives the late comedian high praise by describing him as the only one to do something new in the last 30 years. Others, Chris believes, are following someone else, and Chris includes himself.

Chris may be following someone else, but he also offers a brand new '90s style of humor. This is how it plays out.

Enter Chris Rock:

White people don't understand rap.

That's good. It's not for white people.

Anyway, it's not that complicated. Rap is to black people what country music is to whites. Rap is not made for anyone but the people it's made for. When Garth Brooks makes an album, he doesn't stop and think, "Okay, we need something for the black audience." He just makes his records for the country fan. Travis Tritt doesn't think of yuppies, he thinks of cowboy hats.

Same thing with rappers.

White people: the music's not for you.

You can listen, but don't complain.

Or

A guy on the radio the other day was saying, "We need after-school centers because the kids don't have a place to go play ball. And that's when bad things happen."

Whatever happened to just being bored? When I was a kid we were just plain bored. And we didn't shoot anybody. Can't kids be bored anymore?

No, they need sports.

Now, midnight basketball is the hot thing.

We've got to offer midnight basketball or there's going to be some crime.

What happened to getting some sleep so you could go look for a job in the morning? What about that program?

I missed the job interview—but I scored forty-five!

The audience breaks up.

Exit Chris Rock

2

BED STUY BEAT

❧

SEVERAL ELEMENTS CAN combine to create a solid and original comedy routine—style, technique, ethnic background, and the society of the times in which a comedian lives and works. Chris Rock has developed a unique style and technique of his own. He was, however, born into his ethnic background and the turbulent society of the 1960s, an unforgettable decade in the history of modern America.

Tragedy and turmoil characterized the 1960s, beginning with the assassination of President John F. Kennedy in Dallas, Texas, in 1963. The war in Viet Nam escalated, and the civil rights movement gained momentum. Both divided the nation as television brought home to people the horrors of the war and the violence directed against those in the civil rights movement. African Americans staged sit-ins in the South to defy segregation laws and were arrested. "Freedom riders," both black and white, who rode south to integrate public facilities were attacked and beaten. Riots followed in Mississippi when James Meredith, a black student, tried to enroll at the University of Mississippi, and federal troops were called in to restore order. Violence escalated when four little girls were killed in a bomb attack on a black church in Birmingham, Alabama. Although there was a public outcry from stunned viewers when police

Led by Martin Luther King Jr. (front, second from right), civil rights marchers gather to challenge segregation and the unequal treatment of people of color. Chris Rock was born in the turbulent decade of the 1960s, and learned all about the pain of prejudice and racism as a boy growing up in Brooklyn's Bedford Stuyvesant ghetto.

in Birmingham turned water hoses and dogs on peaceful demonstrators, further conflict broke out.

Across the United States, cities erupted in violence. In 1965, in the Watts section of Los Angeles, one of the worst race riots in U.S. history broke out. Before it was over, 34 people had died, and property damage was more than $200 million. Detroit, Michigan, Newark, New Jersey, Chicago, and New York City were also scenes of riots. Along with riots came the murders of black leaders and civil rights workers. In 1963 Medgar Evers was gunned down in front of his home by a white racist in Mississippi. Three civil rights workers were also murdered the following year, and in 1965, the militant black leader Malcolm X was assassinated as he gave a speech in Harlem in New York City. The assassinations culminated in 1968 with the murders of Martin Luther King Jr. and Robert F. Kennedy, brother of the slain president, who had espoused the cause of civil rights.

It did not appear to be an auspicious decade in which to be born. Nevertheless, on February 7, 1966, Julius and Rose Rock welcomed the first of their seven children, a son they named Chris, who was born in nearby Georgetown Memorial Hospital in Georgetown, South Carolina. Julius drove a truck, and Rose tended to the home in Andrews, South Carolina, a small town about 60 miles from Charleston. The town has not grown much since Chris was born. According to the current police chief, Albert Williams, the population in 1999 numbered around 4,000. People farm or work in the local industries—a paper mill, a steel mill, and a clothing factory. Some commute to Charleston to work in the shipyards.

Crime is relatively low in Andrews, although Chief Williams admits to something of a drug problem in the '90s, and there were two murders. Most adults spend their spare time hunting and fishing, and much like small towns across the nation, the kids are mostly involved in sports. Chief Williams says

Chris, a slim, smallish teenager was the victim of discrimination when he attended an all-white high school in Brooklyn. The taunts and beatings by other students became such an everyday affair that he dropped out at the age of 17.

Andrews is a fine place to live. He does understand, however, why some residents move away to the North, to the big cities in search of better economic opportunities.

The Rocks were one of those families that wanted a better life. In 1972, with six-year-old Chris and his two younger brothers, Andre and Tony, Julius and Rose Rock moved north. The family settled in Brooklyn, a borough of New York City, and made their first home in an apartment in the Crown

Chris's mom presents a plate of good home cooking. Rose Rock raised and cared for seven children as well as scores of foster children in the Rock home. Her influence taught Chris the value of sharing with others while his father taught him the importance of hard work and discipline.

Heights section. They then moved to a brownstone house on Decatur Street in Bedford Stuyvesant, known by residents and nonresidents alike as "Bed Stuy." According to Chris, Bed Stuy is one of the original ghettos, which also include Harlem in New York City's Manhattan borough and the Watts section of Los Angeles. When Chris was growing up in Bed Stuy, it was primarily a black neighborhood, and it still is. Words that describe the community and its vibrant lifestyle are written in a children's picture book called *Bed Stuy Beat:*

Gotta move to the Bed Stuy beat.
Gotta groove to the Bed Stuy beat.
All the action is in the street.
That's where it's at.

As in so many large urban neighborhoods, the action really was in the streets. And the streets of Bed Stuy did not have a good reputation. For unsuspecting youngsters, as well as adults, trouble lurked on the sidewalks and the street corners. Drug dealers pushed their wares, the numbers games appropriated a great deal of money from people who could ill afford it, and youth gangs roamed the neighborhood. Chris knew kids who got into trouble with drugs and the law. His own half brother, a child of his father's first marriage, was, in Chris's words, "in jail a lot."

Too many people were crowded into too small a space. Good jobs were scarce, and scores of residents lived on the edge of poverty. Although Julius Rock was employed driving a newspaper delivery truck, the family, which grew to include four more Rocks, Brian, Kenny, Andrea, and Jordan, had a hard time making ends meet. Chris recalls his mother traveling far out of her way to save a few pennies on groceries or clothes for the kids.

As did many other people in the community, the Rocks often took in foster children, partly because they cared and partly because they needed the money. New York City's foster-care system pays families to take in children who may not have any parents or whose parents are not capable of rearing their children in a decent environment. Foster care is usually a temporary solution until the city makes other arrangements. Chris admits that the Rock household got pretty crowded at times. He also says that his mother treated the foster children as if they were her own. As he relates it: "I'd come home from school some days and see a strange kid in the yard. The kid would say, 'You're my brother,' and I'd ask, 'Who are you you?'"

Rose Rock also remembers those days. "We had a

whole group of foster kids," she explains. "People complimented us then on our [own] kids, and we wanted to give others that chance. The chance to be raised in our home. It took a lot of effort and time. It helped our kids as well. It helped our kids to see that others needed help and to know they could share."

Chris remembers, however, that not every family in the neighborhood who took in foster children treated them with the care his mother gave. Some went out of their way to let those kids know they were "apart" from the others. They might make them sleep in a basement room or serve them different food. Chris recalls one neighbor who admonished him not to drink the juice on the front shelf of her refrigerator because that was "foster kid juice."

Despite the perils of living in Bed Stuy, Chris stayed out of trouble. Decatur Street, which he describes as "the nicest block in the neighborhood," was his oasis. Although as a comedian, he may draw material from the streets of his old neighborhood, the real influence on his early life was within his home. As Rose Rock has put it: "Bed Stuy is what you make it. You have to raise the family with the right values. Send some people to Beverly Hills and if you don't raise them right and their attitude isn't right, they'll go wrong." His mother's ideas have prompted Chris to characterize her as a "ghetto snob." It is not a disparaging comment. Chris is complimenting his mother by pointing out that she did not raise her children to believe they were as good as anyone else. She brought them up to believe they were *better*.

Chris's father, Julius, also had his own ideas about bringing up his children. He was a fanatical disciplinarian, who would not tolerate any disrespect or disobedience, often enforcing his rules with his belt. As Chris has explained. "I always said 'My mother is the president, my father is the troops.' If you messed up, she'd send in the troops. I never got a beating for a bad grade. If I talked back to a teacher, It was *over*—

he'd tear my behind up." When asked how long Julius Rock continued to be a disciplinarian, Chris laughed and said "Until he died." And he adds, "I might even have got smacked at 20."

Chris does not in any way resent his father's punishments. On the contrary, he believes strongly that parents should not coddle their children. His father's discipline, he maintains, helped prepare him for a harsh adult world. In his irreverent fashion, he dismisses the notion that parents should talk to their children rather than smack them. "That's all nonsense," he says. "That's not gonna happen to you in the real world. People aren't gonna *talk* to you—they're trying to *kill* you. You show me a guy who hasn't got beaten up, and I'll show you a guy who needs a beating."

A great many people would find that idea offensive. Undoubtedly, they are not aware of just how much Julius Rock influenced his son and how much Chris cared for his father. Julius died in 1988, at 55, of complications from an ulcer. Chris believes that the stress of overwork and worry about the family helped to kill his father at an early age. Chris and his family still have not recovered from their loss. "We still talk about him like he's here," Chris has said. He smiles as he thinks about Julius and adds, "I remember one of the pieces of advice he gave me. Dad said never to be the smartest guy in the room. You never learn anything that way."

Chris is determined not to go the route his father followed. His mother has moved back to Andrews, South Carolina, and he sometimes thinks about what life would be like if the family had stayed there. He doubts, however, that he would have followed a career in comedy if he had grown up in Andrews. As it turned out, he grew up in New York City, and for someone who at a young age had an eye on show business, there is no better place.

3

THE TOUGH TIMES

— ❧ —

AS A RESULT of the civil rights movement and the slow decline of desegregation, Julius and Rose Rock made a decision that would greatly influence Chris's young life. The events of the '60s and '70s encouraged many African Americans like the Rocks to believe that education for their children would improve with the integration of schools. What they could not foresee was the struggle that would ensue over the decision of the Supreme Court that segregation in the nation's schools violated the U.S. Constitution.

It began in Topeka, Kansas, in 1954, when a railroad worker, Oliver Brown, filed a suit against the city's school board for refusing to allow his daughter Linda to attend a school near the Brown's home. The school was all white, and the segregation laws of the state ruled that black children had to attend separate and supposedly "equal" all-black schools. To Oliver Brown's amazement, the issue became nationwide when the National Association for the Advancement of Colored People (NAACP) stepped in and took the case to the Supreme Court.

Thurgood Marshall, attorney for the NAACP and later a justice on the Supreme Court, challenged the existing doctrine of "separate but equal" facilities for African Americans, which had existed since 1896. Marshall argued that separate facilities were

Beginning in the 1950s, African Americans struggled to overturn segregation in schools and other public places. While thousands marched and demonstrated for equal rights, NAACP attorneys petitioned the courts case by case. Here, a smiling coed, Authorine Lucy (center), leaves the courthouse with her attorneys, Thurgood Marshall (second from left) and Arthur Shores (right center), after the court ruled that Lucy must be readmitted to the all-white University of Alabama, which had denied her admission.

never equal and that such a doctrine was unconstitutional. The Court agreed and ruled that such segregation was henceforth illegal. In handing down the unanimous decision, Chief Justice Earl Warren declared the following: "We conclude that in the field of public education the doctrine of 'separate but equal' has no place. Separate educational facilities are inherently unequal." The following year, 1955, the Court also ruled that desegregation must proceed with "all deliberate speed."

The decades-long discriminatory system of education in the United States was wiped out. Unfortunately, the ruling was only on paper. The Supreme Court does not have the authority or power to enforce its decisions. It is the job of the executive branch of the government, headed by the president, to carry out the Court's rulings. What followed were years of bitter, often violent, confrontation as Americans of the prosperous, peaceful 1950s were faced with some shocking realities. Thanks to television, they could see soldiers escort black children to previously all-white schools and watch as many Southern leaders vowed to fight the Court's ruling and maintain segregation.

It was not only the Supreme Court's decision that helped spark the troubled times. In the same year that the Court ordered desegregation to proceed, a 41-year-old seamstress named Rosa Parks boarded a bus in Montgomery, Alabama, on December 1, and took a seat in the back, where blacks were forced to sit. When "white" seats in the front of the bus became completely filled, Parks and three other black riders were told to give up their seats and stand. Rosa Parks was tired, however, and her feet hurt. When the other black riders got up, she sat stone-faced in her seat. Warned by the driver to move, she quietly defied him with one word, "No." When the driver threatened her with arrest, she replied, "You may do that."

Much later, Parks recalled that she did not think about the consequences of her act. "If I had," she said,

"I might have gotten off the bus." But she did not, and her arrest triggered one of the most dramatic, and effective, demonstrations of nonviolent civil protest in the nation's history. While she was fingerprinted and held for a few hours until a bond was posted, civil rights leaders in Montgomery made a fateful decision. They would use Parks's defiance to challenge the segregation laws, and their weapon would be a boycott of the city's entire bus system.

Montgomery leaders called in a 26-year-old minister from Atlanta, Georgia, named Martin Luther King Jr. to help organize and lead the boycott. It

Breaking an Alabama law that segregated bus riders, Rosa Parks of Montgomery refused to give up her seat to a white rider. Her arrest and fingerprinting triggered one of the most effective protests of the civil rights movement—the year-long boycott of the city's bus system.

For leading and taking part in the bus boycott in Montgomery, Alabama, Martin Luther King Jr. was also arrested. Along with King and Rosa Parks, some 100 people were charged with breaking the segregation laws.

was a formidable challenge, for how would African Americans get to jobs, stores, and churches without public transportation? The answer was that more than 20,000 black citizens formed car pools, hired taxis, rode bicycles, or just walked. Intimidation did not deter them. Many car poolers were regularly stopped by city police who hoped to find some infraction of traffic rules. King himself was arrested for driving 30 miles an hour in a 25-mile zone. When he was jailed, the supporting crowd outside grew so large that the authorities released him.

The Montgomery boycott lasted more than a year—381 days—and ended in victory for the black citizens of Montgomery. The city could not afford the loss of so many riders. More important for the civil rights movement itself, the Supreme Court declared that bus segregation was illegal. When that news arrived, King boarded a city bus, deposited his 15 cents, and sat in a formerly "white only" seat.

The struggle for equality was far from over, however. In many parts of the nation, the confrontations were real and often terrifying. It seemed that because of the prejudices of so many whites, civil rights and equal protection under the law for black Americans would be a long time coming. Governor Herman Talmadge of Georgia voiced the attitude of many whites when he said in 1954, "I do not believe in Negroes and whites associating with each other socially or in our school system, and as long as I am governor, it won't happen."

Talmadge's resistance was echoed by fellow governor Orval Faubus of Arkansas when in 1957 he defied the ruling of the Supreme Court, precipitating what became a national crisis. Cameras settled on Little Rock's Central High School in a working-class neighborhood as nine African-American children attempted to integrate the school. Faubus vowed it would never happen. Giving his reasons, he concluded that admitting black children to the school would incite violence. He declared that busloads of segregationists were advancing on Little Rock to surround the school and that white mothers were preparing to protect their own children at Central High. Stores, he said, were reporting a run on the sale of knives, and both black and white high-school students in the city were carrying guns. Under the circumstances, Faubus reasoned, it was necessary to call in the Arkansas National Guard. They would function, he insisted, "not as segregationists nor integrationists, but as soldiers to carry out their assigned tasks."

Most television viewers were shocked as they watched the situation unfold. Nine neatly dressed, frightened black children walked slowly to the steps of Central High to be confronted by the pointed rifles of the guard. The violence that Faubus had threatened could now become a reality. Mobs of threatening segregationists roamed the school and the city, and for their own safety, all black students were ordered to stay home. In desperation, Little Rock's mayor called Washington for help. President Dwight Eisenhower was reluctant to intervene, but he had no choice, and he finally ordered federal troops to Little Rock to restore order.

Central High became a virtual armed camp as U.S. soldiers surrounded the school to protect the "Central High Nine" as they finally attended classes. Whites, adults and youth alike, taunted the children and indulged in name calling to intimidate them. Chastened by the federal troops' show of force, however, whites finally backed down. But Governor Faubus was not ready to concede. In 1958 he closed Little Rock's schools, and they did not open again until later in 1959 following a Supreme Court ruling to integrate.

Despite the Little Rock ruling, public schools were still not easily integrated. In 1962, the University of Mississippi refused to register James Meredith, an African-American veteran, as a student. Governor Ross Barnett personally blocked his way in defiance of a federal court order. When the Mississippi National Guard was unable to protect Meredith from angry mobs, President John F. Kennedy ordered 5,000 federal troops to the state. Meredith had to be guarded until he graduated a year later.

Governor George Wallace of Alabama tried the same tactic the following year. Taking his cue from Governor Barnett, Wallace made his famous "stand in the schoolhouse door," attempting to block African-American students from entering the University of Alabama. Wallace backed off, however, when President Kennedy sent federal officials to confront the recalcitrant governor.

As the '60s progressed, the civil rights movement continued to pressure the federal government to pursue equality for all citizens. A constitutional

amendment outlawed the poll tax, a fee Southern states made voters pay in order to vote. Since many blacks were too poor to pay the tax, thousands were prevented from voting. Literacy tests for voting were also banned. A voting rights act strengthened the federal government's enforcement of the rights of African Americans and other minorities to vote, and legislation by Congress banned discrimination in housing. In 1964, Congress passed the most far-reaching

Two federal officers accompany four of the "Central High Nine" students as they leave Central High School. Because of the threat of violence from segregationists, the black students who attempted to integrate the school had to be escorted to and from their classes.

civil rights act since the Civil War. The act banned discrimination in employment, public facilities, and in programs funded by the federal government. It also set up the Equal Employment Opportunity Commission, which works to stamp out job-related discrimination.

To promote further integration in public education, laws allowed students to be bused out of their neighborhoods to other schools where the educational facilities might be better. A well-intended idea, it was opposed by many, both white and black. People believed that integrated schools would lead to integrated neighborhoods, and whites especially feared the loss of property values if that happened.

Arguments like these helped destroy peace in neighborhoods and relations among neighbors. In the early 1970s in the Canarsie section of Brooklyn, a rabbi who was taking part in a protest march was questioned by the reporters. He was asked, "As a spiritual leader, what do you think of this controversy?" Speaking into the television cameras, he replied honestly, saying that segregation was wrong and that children were more important than property. For this courageous stand, his family was harassed, and he was driven from his position, his home, and his neighborhood. Such scenes were repeated many times over—in different forms and with different people—throughout the United States.

Such incidents did not discourage Julius and Rose Rock—at least at the outset. They decided that instead of attending P.S. 277 in Bed Stuy, Chris should be bused to a white school. Rose Rock later explained their thinking. "At that time, it was a mind set," she said. "White was better. It wasn't always true, but it was a belief of the times. White kids had better education, schools, teachers. So, that's where Chris went." Beginning in the second grade, Chris was bused to P.S. 22 in the Gerritson Beach section of Brooklyn, which was a white community that was

Young Chris had a miserable time attending school outside his neighborhood. Although his parents felt that a white school would provide a better education, Chris recalls that "it was an awful school, and I did horribly."

just about as poor as Bed Stuy.

The good intentions of Chris's parents did not turn out as they had hoped. Instead of a better school, Chris recalls vividly that what he got was a worse education in a worse neighborhood than his own. He also suffered from all the prejudices that had characterized the worst times of the '60s. The only black kid in his class, he was taunted every day with racial slurs. His tormentors spit at him and beat him up. The treatment never stopped.

"Nobody wanted to talk to me," he recalled years later. "The girls. Nothing. I try to forget all about that." Chris has said that the situation was so tough that he did not learn to tie his own shoes until he was nine years old.

In time, Chris withdrew into himself during school hours. The real Chris Rock remained hidden from nine o'clock to three. Only at home could he be himself and show his potential as a comedian in the making, a skinny kid who looked younger than his years and cracked jokes to amuse his family and bring on laughter.

If Chris's life in elementary school was bad, it was even worse at James Madison High School, which was also away from his own neighborhood. The brutal teasing and beatings continued. He couldn't beat the others and he couldn't join them. So he finally refused to return. At the age of 17, he informed his parents that he was dropping out of school. Chris recalls, "I said [to my parents] 'I'm not going back. Beat me, whatever you want to do—I ain't going back.'" Chris's experiences did not make him a supporter of desegregation. He has remarked that "if I didn't get bused to school, I'd be, like, normal."

Chris's parents supported his decision. They may have been disappointed, but Rose Rock is proud of her son and the way he weathered those bad years. She recalls that he would say, "I'm Chris Rock" in a firm voice. "He had a strong sense of identity," she explains, "of self-esteem, of who he was. We always let him and the others know that they were very important to us. That gave them self-confidence. One time our son Andre had to complete this sentence in school: 'My Mom says I am _____.' The other kids wrote things like 'a slob' or 'late to dinner,' but Andre wrote, 'My Mom says I'm the best thing that ever happened.' I never forgot that."

Rose Rock is also proud of the fact that her eldest son never became involved in drugs or crime. She

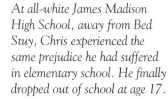

At all-white James Madison High School, away from Bed Stuy, Chris experienced the same prejudice he had suffered in elementary school. He finally dropped out of school at age 17.

believes that Chris had too much self-respect for that. Her other children met her expectations too. Andre taught school for a time and now owns a trucking company. Tony works on Wall Street and is also a stand-up comic who has worked at the same club where Chris got his start. Brian is in television production, and Kenny is at New York University. Andrea, a teenager, is an honor student, and the youngest, Jordan, is acknowledged by his mother to be a "a sports freak."

Although Chris could not foresee the future, his decision to drop out marked the beginning of a career in the world of comedy. Rose expresses some surprise that Chris became a comedian. "I thought maybe he'd be a journalist," she remarks. "He was always good at writing. He could take 10 spelling words and make them into a two-page story." Chris himself has said that he had the notion he might like to write for the television sitcom *The Jeffersons*.

As a stand-up comic, Chris can now take words and weave them into his routines, in which he often refers to his hated school years and brings a special slant to ideas about education. Although Chris later got a General Equivalency Diploma (GED), which is supposed to be equal to a high-school diploma and provide the chance to go on to higher education, he is not impressed. He calls the GED "nonsense" and takes a poke at what he calls a second-rate piece of paper, labeling it "Good Enough Diploma." He scoffs, "I don't get it. How can you make up four years in a six-hour exam and then think people are right when they say, 'Now you can go to college.'?"

Continuing his take on education, Chris reveals just how painful his school years were. Relating education to television, he points to shows that depict the smart kid as the oddball, someone you would least want to be around. As far as Chris is concerned, television promotes an "anti-education thing" and is worse than the much-criticized violence and profanity often shown. Chris has also refused to give money to relatives or friends who want to get started in show business. He tells them he will, however, give them college tuition. That way, if they fail in the entertainment world, they can be successful in the academic world.

In another routine, Chris talks about meeting a former classmate some 15 years after he dropped out. Returning home from a trip to Los Angeles, Chris hired a limousine from the airport. Who should be driving but a guy who had tormented him daily at school. Chris relates that at first he felt the same old fear from past years. The driver, however, acted as if they were the world's best friends. He gushed to Chris how he told all his friends that he had gone to school with Chris Rock.

When Chris arrived home, he gave the driver a big tip because, as Chris put it, he knew it "would mess with his mind." Never getting the drift, the driver handed Chris his card and indicated they might hang out together.

Chris thought, "Why would I ever want to hang out with you?"

Later, when he got over his anger, Chris realized what was happening: "This guy and I had just been playing our roles. He was a white boy. I was some black in an all-white school. It was his job to treat me like dirt.

"Okay. No hard feelings."

4

WHAT IS COMEDY?

— ❦ —

Grinning and gesturing, Chris emphasizes his point during one of his routines. His frank and in-your-face style of stand-up comedy, before a live audience or in front of a camera, has brought him success and widespread popularity.

IN MODERN TIMES, people think of comedy as entertainment meant to amuse. The word comes from the Greek term *komos*, which means to "revel" or "sing." Through the centuries, however, its meaning has varied. All kinds of comedies have been written, performed, and watched. Comedy can have many different meanings.

In the Middle Ages, comedy was simply a story with a happy ending. The Italian poet Dante titled his epic work *The Divine Comedy*. The story of the poet's journey through hell and purgatory is not humorous. The ending, however, is joyful as it culminates in Paradise. Later, William Shakespeare became the master of romantic comedy (as well as drama), tales of troubles that eventually end in the triumph of love. Shakespeare's merry romp in *A Midsummer Night's Dream* is full of terrible mishaps, pranks, and magic spells at the end of which true love prevails.

When a work ridicules the social customs or traditions of a place or era, it is a comedy of manners. Probably the greatest playwright in this genre was Jean Baptiste Poquelin, better known as Molière. He poked fun at the pretensions of 17th-century French society in such works as *The School for Wives* and *The Misanthrope*. The former tells of a man who wants his beloved raised in total innocence so that she will

Musical comedy is a purely American development and in one form or another has been a mainstay of the theater world since the mid-19th century. Shown here is a scene from Show Boat, *considered the first "modern" musical because it used music so well to tell a story.*

remain ever faithful to him, a reflection of the common notion of the time that high-class women had to be kept nearly in seclusion. The precautions are ineffective, however; she is swept away by another. In *The Misanthrope*, the hero vows to be completely honest and ignore the conventions of a hypocritical society. To his dismay, the woman he loves refuses to give up her position and rebuffs him.

Modern times brought the genre known as musical comedy, or simply "musicals," stage productions that combine music and dance to tell a story. A truly American invention, musicals are the nation's great contribution to the theater. Historians credit a play called *The Black Crook*, which opened on Broadway in 1866, as the first musical. Although *The Black Crook* was popular in its time, it was not until the turn of the 20th century that musical theater grabbed public attention. In 1903, composer Victor Herbert launched the first of his "operettas," *Babes in Toyland*. Romantic, usually light, comedies with singable songs, Herbert's operettas, and those of other similar composers, were immensely popular, and are still performed today.

A performer who is considered one of the giants of musical comedy was George M. Cohan. A talented song-and-dance man, Cohan wrote, produced, and starred in his own musicals, introducing such enduring songs as "I'm a Yankee Doodle Dandy" and "Give My Regards to Broadway." Another giant was Florenz Ziegfeld, who staged lavish shows called the *Follies*. Ziegfeld's specialty was beautiful showgirls in extravagant costumes who glided around the stage as singers and dancers performed. He also harked back to the older days of vaudeville in presenting variety shows in which comedians were included. Stars such as Will Rogers, Fanny Brice, and Eddie Cantor were introduced to the public by Ziegfeld.

Musicals became much more sophisticated when George and Ira Gershwin entered the scene with their first show, *Funny Face*, in 1927. The Gershwins' scores, and the stories, in such musicals as *Lady Be Good* and *Of Thee I Sing* were more complex and clever than light musical comedy. Other musicals still entertained audiences with songs, dancing, and comedy, however. For instance, the show *No! No! Nanette* wowed audiences with its spectacular tap dancing.

According to theater historians, the first truly "modern" musical appeared in 1927 when Jerome Kern and Oscar Hammerstein II wrote *Show Boat*. The story of a troupe of performers who moved up and down the Mississippi River in their paddle-wheel boat tells of lost love and renewed love among the characters. *Show Boat* is modern because it merged the songs and the story so successfully. And in doing so it gave the nation the memorable song "Old Man River," performed by the incomparable African-American singer Paul Robeson.

The period from the 1920s through the 1950s was probably the richest for the Broadway musical. Cole Porter, Irving Berlin, and partners Richard Rodgers and Oscar Hammerstein II wrote show after show. For Rodgers and Hammerstein, their first success was *Oklahoma!* in 1943. It was another first in musicals through its incredible choreography that was so completely integrated into the story. Rodgers and Hammerstein went on to thrill audiences with their music in *South Pacific*, *The King and I*, and their last musical in 1959, *The Sound of Music*.

Musicals took on yet another aspect when in 1957, the collaboration of composer and conductor Leonard Bernstein, choreographer Jerome Robbins, and songwriter Stephen Sondheim produced *West Side Story*. An updated version of *Romeo and Juliet*, the show introduced true tragedy into the American musical. In 1956, Alan Jay Lerner and Frederick Loewe introduced the classic story of the flower girl who finds love with a cranky professor in *My Fair Lady* (based on a play by George Bernard Shaw). They followed that hit in 1960 with the story of King Arthur and the Round Table in *Camelot*.

Musical comedy was by no means totally extinct, however. It just took on another form, which as it progressed into later decades, included less comedy and, for some critics, less good music. The first major show of this genre was the rock musical *Hair*, which opened on Broadway in 1968. Billed as "An American Tribal Love-Rock Musical," it was also the first mainstream musical to feature nudity. Another rock musical, *The Wiz*, based on *The Wizard of Oz*, appeared in 1975 with an all-black cast.

Musicals became more complex and in-depth in such productions as Stephen Sondheim's *Company* and *Into the Woods*, which was based on a fairy tale.

Those who wanted horror in their musicals flocked to see *Sweeney Todd, The Demon Barber of Fleet Street*, which was about a self-styled murderer who revenged wrongs by killing his customers and grinding them up into meat pies. It was, however, the advent of the grand epics mostly based on fictional stories that dominated the '80s and '90s. Beginning in 1981 with *Cats*, based on stories by poet T. S. Eliot, musicals became huge productions with elaborate stage effects and, some would complain, not too many singable numbers. It appeared that just about anything could be a subject for musicals. *The Phantom of the Opera, Dr. Jekyll and Mr. Hyde, Les Miserables*, and *The Scarlet Pimpernel* are among this genre. They cannot really be called comedies, but they are billed as musicals.

Another form of comedy, quite different from musicals, is "black comedy." The expression does not refer to the routines delivered by Chris Rock, Bill Cosby, or Whoopi Goldberg. It is comedy with a pessimistic side, and it is meant to make people see and feel that life is a complex mixture of humor and sadness. Often presented through satire, black comedy attempts to reveal the darker part of human society. The great Charlie Chaplin did it in his 1947 film *Monsieur Verdoux*. An ordinary, respectable family man who is unfairly fired from his job goes on a murderous rampage, pretending to marry and then killing rich widows for their money so he can support an ailing wife and little son. Many of the scenes in which Chaplin tries but fails to murder a woman are hilarious, but the theme is not. The film expressed Chaplin's view of a callous society that destroys a man and then executes him for crimes he was driven to commit.

Another black comedy was the 1970 film *Catch 22*, adapted from Joseph Heller's novel of the same title. It tells of a soldier caught between the horrors of war and the hilarious blunders of the military. Since publication of the novel and release of the film, the

It seemed that no one would ever surpass Charlie Chaplin and his comic talent, expressed so often through his role as the Little Tramp. City Lights, *a silent film with a musical score composed by Chaplin, is considered by many to be his masterpiece. Here the Little Tramp wistfully contemplates a water fountain that does not appear to be working.*

term "Catch 22" has become part of the language, indicating a situation that will surely trip you up no matter what you do.

No matter what the differences are in various kinds of comedy, the word "comedy" or "comic" still conjures up certain images. It may be a funny person delivering snappy lines to a live audience or a cast in a situation comedy that draws laughter. It certainly can be comedians in films, in which so many "greats" have performed.

Called by an early colleague "the greatest artist

who ever lived," Charles Spencer "Charlie" Chaplin began his comedy career in England. Born in 1889 to a mother who was a music-hall entertainer, Chaplin himself was on the stage at the age of five. By the time he was 17, he had joined a touring company where he learned his basic comic skills. Chaplin entered the Hollywood scene in the silent-film era, which began in the late 1890s and continued until talking pictures appeared in the late 1920s. Chaplin created what some have called "a universal folk hero" in his lovable, naïve, often sad Little Tramp character. In his short comedies and feature films, Chaplin depicted what he considered a soulless modern society bent on destroying the individual. From such material, Chaplin could draw laughter as well as tears. Although honored with accolades for his films, Chaplin's morals were questioned because of a scandal involving a young woman. He left the United States and in 1953 settled in Switzerland. In the greatly changed atmosphere of the '70s, he returned to Hollywood as an elderly man to receive a special Academy Award for his contributions to comedy.

Often compared with Chaplin was Joseph Francis "Buster" Keaton, who also gained fame in silent films. The son of vaudeville entertainers, Keaton mastered the timing and pratfalls of his craft while still a child. Billed as "the human mop" because his parents wiped up the floor with him, Keaton was so skilled at comic tricks that many people thought he was a midget. When he grew up, however, his trademark was his pained, never-smiling face. Keaton played to perfection the deadpan character who is constantly in conflict with mechanical monsters, and film viewers roared with laughter. In making people laugh, Keaton said, "The thing is not to be ridiculous. . . . Sometimes I'm in the middle of building a gag that turns out to be ridiculous. So, well, we have to think of something else. Sit it out."

Keaton's career declined in the 1920s when talkies changed the film industry. He did return, however, for an appearance in *Sunset Boulevard* (1950) and *It's a Mad, Mad, Mad, Mad World* (1963).

In performing stand-up comedy, Chris Rock is following in the footsteps of many great comedians. Their styles and deliveries vary, but they are masters of monologues, jokes, and gags, which are the hallmarks of stand-up comics.

Chris is not the first stand-up comedian to deliver "politically incorrect" material in a raucous and often shocking style. In the late 1950s and until his death in 1966, Lenny Bruce stunned mainstream audiences with his raging routines attacking organized religion, racism, and hypocrisy. He would sometimes stumble and mumble his way across a stage, muttering obscenities, and then suddenly shout out his punch line. Bruce was a master of timing, and often made up his routines as he went along. He did not hesitate to tell the truth as he saw it, and many consider him a hero of free speech.

Chris also admires George Carlin, a comedian whose style has been compared to that of Lenny Bruce. But Carlin began his career in the clubs and on television in the '60s as a somewhat conventional stand-up comic known for his spoofs and lampoons of radio and television shows. Then, in the '70s, Carlin changed his routines. He took on the cloak of social activist and began satirizing what he considered the self-righteousness and phoniness of society. He especially targeted pop culture and the media. Moving around the stage, Carlin shouted four-letter words as he delivered his stinging monologues.

Although Carlin's popularity with mainstream audiences declined in the '80s, he made a comeback in the early '90s with an HBO special in which he challenged his audience once again, rattling off tirades against everything from clichés in language to environmentalists to the Miss America Pageant. Many critics have noted that Carlin's counterculture style has influenced a whole generation of stand-up comics, and that includes Chris Rock.

Another comedian whose style Chris has studied is Don Rickles, who is considered the king of "insult comedy." He began in the nightclub scene in the 1950s, and although he has appeared in films in recent years as a serious actor, he still performs in clubs in Las Vegas and Atlantic City. Rickles does not take on social issues. Rather, his style is to deliver snappy one-liners and hurl such insults as "hockey puck" and "dummy" at members of his audience. Unlike Bruce, however, Rickles is not hostile, and his audiences do not seem to mind being insulted with humor.

Woody Allen has been in the spotlight, particularly with his many films, since the early '60s. He began his career writing gags for television shows, during which he showed a remarkable gift for one-liners, a talent he admired in his role models Bob Hope and Groucho Marx. Allen soon switched to performing his own material in 1960 in a small New York nightclub. He caught on, and throughout the '60s, he was widely popular in clubs and on television. Allen did not favor political or social-issue comedy. His routines were personal, as he poked fun at himself, the nerdy little guy who is always being put down and never seems to have luck with women. In the mid-'60s, Allen turned to films and began writing, directing, and playing in his own movies. Like his comedy, Allen's films are very personal, expressing subjects he has dwelled on throughout his career: sex, death, and the meaning of life.

An African-American comedian named Dick Gregory combined humor and social commentary in his shows during the 1960s, much as Chris Rock does today. Gregory had dropped out of Southern Illinois University in the mid-1950s and joined the army; while serving in the military, he became interested in entertainment as a profession. Within a few years, he was one of the most popular comics of his day. A lot of Dick Gregory's material was based on his participation in the civil rights movement and on his opposition to the Vietnam War. By the end of the decade, Gregory had taken up a full-time role as an activist, even running for president in 1968 for the Peace and Freedom Party. He has supported anti-drug campaigns, fought hunger, and worked for world peace and for the rights of African Americans and Native Americans.

While Dick Gregory was discussing uncomfortable subjects in his comedy routines, another African-American comedian was also becoming popular: Bill Cosby. Although Gregory is no longer an entertainer, Cosby has continued delighting audiences since the 1960s with his squeaky clean, family-style humor. Like Chris Rock, Cosby began his career as a stand-up comedian in nightclubs. He came to nationwide attention on television with the programs *I Spy* in the '60s and later *The Cosby Show*, a sitcom that was one of the biggest TV hits of the '80s and '90s. He is still going strong today with his new comedy, *Cosby*, in which he portrays a cranky grandfather. Cosby's humor is quiet, thoughtful, and warm, and audiences smile with him rather than laugh out loud.

In thinking about black comedians, one of the first who probably springs into people's minds is Eddie Murphy, the man who gave Chris his first big break. Murphy began his career as a stand-up comic in clubs when he was 15. Then, in 1980, at 19, he joined *Saturday Night Live*. A great impersonator, Murphy's talent was in delivering spoofs of famous people. He satirized Bill Cosby and the exercise-diet spokesman Richard Simmons, as well as Mr. Rogers, host of the well-known children's television show. Murphy later became popular in films such as the *Beverly Hills Cop* series. A critic has described Murphy's comedy as "a kind of sassy self-assurance,

Bill Cosby (right) became famous early in his career when he starred with Robert Culp in the television series I Spy. It was the continuing saga of two espionage agents who obviously use unique methods to catch the wrongdoers.

strangely without malice."

The comedian Caryn Johnson, known to her fans worldwide as Whoopi Goldberg, bows to none in the smartness of her delivery and style. Well known for her biting wit when hosting the Academy Awards, she began her career when she created The Spook Show in Berkeley, California, in 1982. Audiences went wild over her four main "spooks," the slightly offbeat people who suffer the pain and heartache of life in modern society.

One spook, the white "surfer chick" of California, talked like an airhead and lived for the shopping mall. But the comedy turned dark when she became pregnant and alone and very frightened. Another spook, the loudmouth Ph.D and former drug addict Fontaine, was a jive-talking guy who began a monologue of his funny experiences on a plane and wound up talking about the tragedy of Anne Frank. A young disabled woman about to get married was Goldberg's third character. The comedian included this character to show that a disabled person was not someone apart from society. As the character developed, audiences forgot all about the handicap.

Perhaps the most endearing of Goldberg's spooks was the nine-year-old black girl who trooped across the stage with a light shirt draped over her head. She explained that the shirt is her "long blonde tresses" and informed the audience she did not want to be black anymore. She wanted to be white so she could get on the television show *The Love Boat* because everybody on the show has long blonde tresses.

Besides being a successful comic, Goldberg has had phenomenal success in films. She was nominated for an Academy Award for her role as Celie in the film *The Color Purple* (1985), in which she plays the dramatic role of an illiterate young girl in the South who grows into a woman of dignity and maturity. Turning back to comedy in 1992, Goldberg captured audiences with her portrayal of the sassy nightclub singer disguised as a reluctant nun hiding out from the mob in a convent. The film *Sister Act* was a huge hit with audiences and critics alike. As one reporter said, "This is the year Whoopi Goldberg finally became bigger than her hair."

Another black comedian whose work Chris Rock admires tremendously is Richard Pryor. A comic star of nightclubs, Pryor gained wide success on television and later in films. His most amusing characterizations are of streetwise blacks. Pryor laughs at himself as he delivers his lines, amused by what he sees around him and definitely perplexed by it all.

These talented artists of this and earlier times belong to a profession that Chris Rock had wanted to join since he was 17 and dropped out of school. It is, however, a tough profession to crack. An aspiring hopeful trying to break into comedy has a hard road

In her act The Spook Show Whoopi Goldberg won fans with her satiric but understanding portrayal of those who could be considered society's outcasts. Here, the loud-mouthed but soft-hearted Fontaine expresses what's on his mind.

to travel. Effort, energy, patience, and a very thick skin are required to even get to be seen and heard.

Some comedians succeed in films; some break out in television. But Chris wanted to be a stand-up comic, so where could he begin? He, like others, had to find a spot where he could perform before a live audience and deliver his routines. For many, including Chris, comedy clubs are the answer. Among many other cities, New York boasts numerous such clubs that give new talent a chance. Unknown and barely known hopefuls can perform, usually once a week at a time generally called "open-mike night." These clubs include the Comic Strip, where Chris began, Stand Up New York, Caroline's, Don't Tell Mama, New York Comedy Club, Comedy Cellar,

Dick Gregory (left), noted for the social commentary he brought to his comedy, shares the stage with Richard Pryor at Washington's Kennedy Center in 1998. Pryor, who suffers from multiple sclerosis, received the center's Mark Twain Prize.

Gotham, and Dangerfield's, the well-known club operated by comedian Rodney Dangerfield.

Clubs work in different ways with new talent. Some allow a new comic to just walk up and grab the microphone. Others give mike time by lottery, booking slots for acts up to six months in advance. In this approach, the would-be comedians have set "appointments" and plenty of time to prepare—and worry. Some clubs hold auditions before a novice can perform to make certain he or she does not fall flat and turn the act into disaster.

In some clubs, the management is quite clever at packing the house with a paying clientele. They ask performers to bring along their friends. A few clubs make performers pay for the privilege of testing their routines. Would-be comics are often glad to pay the price. Paying such dues means they are "in the loop." They can go on before more established talent and learn the ropes. And they gain exposure, especially if patrons have come to see an up-and-coming entertainer or more well-known person. In effect, if customers want to see the professional, they have to see the novice first. If a newcomer shows any talent at all and the audience is receptive, he or she will be asked to come back. Now the new comic does not have to buy his or her way in or ask friends to tag along. As a veteran of the clubs has put it, "You weasel your way in!"

Chris Rock succeeded in weaseling his way into the limelight. He is now one of the established stars, perhaps the hottest young comedian of the 1990s, and certainly the hottest black comedian.

5

STAND-UP CHRIS

❧

CHRIS ROCK HAS commented that he might not have become a comedian if his family had stayed in Andrews, South Carolina. Perhaps it was life in New York that pushed the slightly built, boyish-looking African American into a career in comedy

After Chris quit high school, there was no question that he would have to earn his own way. His father told him, "You have to work for a living. I don't want you messing with money." But messing with money would not be a concern any time soon, as Chris's start in the working world was not auspicious. The 17-year-old was earning the minimum wage, $3.35 an hour, flipping burgers at a local McDonald's.

Today, Chris Rock does not think much of the minimum wage. In his comedy routines, Chris points out that a boss who will pay minimum wage doesn't care about an employee's family, holidays, or quality of life. It means, he says, a boss who would pay even less if it weren't illegal. At the same time, Chris does not want to see the minimum wage requirements eliminated. If that happened, he claims, some bosses would be sure to take advantage of their employees.

In addition to his stint at MacDonald's, Chris helped his father on the newspaper truck, hauled dishes as a busboy at a restaurant, and worked in a discount store. It was not what Chris had in mind for himself. So the kid who made them laugh at home

At the age of 18, Chris was testing his stand-up routines at the clubs around New York City, and the exposure landed him a spot on Eddie Murphy's cable show Uptown Comedy Express. *He shared the spotlight there with Arsenio Hall (front, left) and (from left to right in the back) Barry Sobel, Marsha Warfield, and Robert Townsend.*

55

It was Eddie Murphy, here in a scene from Beverly Hills Cop II, *who spotted Chris in a club and gave him his first professional gig as a stand-up comic.*

tried his luck at night on the black comedy circuit, honing his skills for something bigger and better.

The bigger and better chance came when he was at the Comic Strip club on open-mike night. When the invitation came to step up and perform, Chris accepted. He says that the first time he was on that stage, he knew he was home. This was where he belonged, and for the first time in his life, he felt he was doing something really good. This, he knew, was his talent. When he stepped off the stage, the manager said, "You passed the audition. You can work as a regular now." Chris had weaseled his way in. He had been initiated into the unique, and sometimes zany, world of stand-up comedy.

Stand-up comedy takes confidence and dedication as well as talent. Appearing live before total strangers and trying to turn staring, sometimes stone faces into smiles and then laughter is a challenge. A song from the 1990s' Broadway musical *Late Nite Comic* expresses just how hard it is to be funny:

> Late nite comic
> Your audience is gone
> But still you grab that microphone
> And still you carry on
> Late nite comic
> Keep the laughter coming till the dawn

Chris still kept his day job, but the stints at the Comic Strip were a start. He was gaining a reputation as a young man with a talent for his routines about race, one of which joked about a white family that moved into Bed Stuy. "Uh-oh," Chris cracked, "here comes the neighborhood." The manager of the club remembers that "he [Chris] didn't really talk about the things that a normal teenager would talk about, such as school or living at home with your parents, even though he did live at home with his parents."

It seemed as if Chris would never go beyond the Comic Strip until one night in 1986, actor-comedian Eddie Murphy dropped by and caught Chris on the stage. Murphy was impressed. In fact, he was so impressed that he later offered Chris a spot on his cable television show *Uptown Comedy Express*.

Murphy also helped Chris get a small role as a parking-lot attendant in Murphy's film *Beverly Hills Cop II*. The film appearance was a small start for which Chris was paid $600 for one scene. He snagged another part in the 1988 film *I'm Gonna Git You Sucka*, a hip spoof of "blaxploitation" films. The term refers to the generally poorly made movies in the 1980s that stereotyped blacks as aggressive, often violent, characters. Chris's performance as a customer in a rib joint attracted the attention of Arsenio Hall, who invited him to appear on his late-night television show. When Lorne Michaels, producer of the popular and successful *Saturday Night Live (SNL)*, saw Chris on Hall's show, he invited the young comedian to audition for his show. Chris passed with flying colors and began his stint on *SNL* in 1990.

Chris is probably best remembered from his *SNL* days for his character called Nat X in the sketch "The Dark Side with Nat X." Wearing hair that resembled an enormous head of black broccoli and sporting a dashiki (a brightly colored African shirt), Chris spoofed the militant black leader Malcolm X. Without a trace of reverence, Chris and his wild hair delivered a lengthy sermon that included such zingers as "Live, from Compton, California, a city so bad it has a drive-by shooting lane." In one sketch, he zeroed in on whites with five reasons why they can't dance:

5. Too busy counting their money.
4. Too busy counting my money.
3. Small thighs make it hard to dip.
2. They're inferior.
1. They can—they're just waiting for the waltz to come back.

Nat X acknowledged that African Americans had gained a Black History Month but pointed out that it is February, the shortest month of the year. Furthermore, it's the coldest month. Nat X figured that month was chosen in case black people wanted to have a parade.

Nat X did not let blacks off the hook either. On one show, he took a jab at Michael Jackson when he asked Jackson's sister LaToya, "The boy got a brain in a jar?" Nat X did not hesitate to confront Jackson personally. On a video hookup with the singer, Nat X led off with the ghetto slur "I'm your father."

Saturday Night Live was the break Chris had been waiting for. Offbeat and nutty, *SNL* was the vehicle

that had launched Eddie Murphy, among other stars, to fame. "It was a dream come true," said Chris when he signed a five-year contract. Some critics claimed that Chris, the first African American hired for the show since 1985, was hired as *SNL*'s token black performer. Others differed. One wrote that Chris would "inject some urban life into a program dominated by church ladies and subterranean heavy-metal heads."

Nevertheless, aside from Nat X, Chris was pretty much in the background. His stand-up delivery with its biting jabs about people, race, politics, and society

Saturday Night Live gave Chris (far left, second row) a chance to perform with an outstanding cast, shown in this 1992 photo. His Nat X sketch, a parody of the militant black leader Malcolm X, was original and popular. But he never made a top spot on the show.

in general was difficult to integrate with the *SNL* format. Through his performances at the Comic Strip, Chris had created a routine that was brutally frank and often raunchy. More than a few objected to his "dirty language." The *Washington Post* criticized him for jokes that "you don't hear except on inner-city playgrounds." Chris was forced to tone down some of his material.

SNL was not Chris's first encounter with criticism. After his appearance on the *Arsenio Hall Show*, both Hall and the show's director, Spike Lee, blasted him for telling jokes inappropriate for television. Chris was further slapped down when after his second appearance with Hall, the talk-show host felt compelled to apologize to the audience for his guest's material.

Chris's style was not the only objection. On *SNL* he often presented an image of being nervous in front of the camera. And he later admitted that he sometimes came to the show unprepared and exhausted from all-night parties that enliven many a newcomer's first taste of fame. "I didn't rehearse seriously enough," he has said. Conan O'Brien, Chris's friend and a writer on *SNL*, realized that Chris was not going to make it on the show. O'Brien commented that what Chris "really needed to do was go off and be Chris Rock and develop his own ideas." In 1993, after three years on *SNL*, and before completing his contract, Chris left the show.

Even before Chris left *SNL*, he had made his third film appearance when he landed a part in the 1991 film *New Jack City*, an antidrug crime movie directed by Mario Van Peebles, a well-respected filmmaker. Chris got good reviews for his performance as Pookie, a crack addict turned informer. Although this film and his previous one did not enter the mainstream, Chris had gained a reputation among blacks. In 1999, when talking about his early career, he said, "I'd been famous in the ghetto for a long time. I did *New Jack City* like 10 years

Chris turned in a dramatic per-formance as a junkie turned informer in the film New Jack City. It was a featured part and he got good reviews for his performance.

ago. I did *I'm Gonna Git You Sucka* 11 years ago. So we're talking, like, most of my life."

In 1993, Chris was cast in the television sitcom *In Living Color*. He appeared in only a few episodes, however, before the show was canceled. Trying to keep busy, he cowrote and starred in *CB4*, a comedy film about forming a rap group. When that fizzled out, Chris returned to the comedy club circuit. Now

With a long wig and clothes too big for his slight frame, Chris appears as a rapper trying to form a group in CB4. The film was his first attempt at writing and coproducing.

his urban, streetwise humor began to garner him a larger audience, and he was earning a reputation as a "hot new comic." Still, it was not the big time, and it was not steady enough work.

Nineteen ninety-six rolled around and Chris Rock had no club dates and no film prospects. He was just another comic on the unemployment line. It was an especially painful time for Chris because, as he freely admits, he is an insecure person. He feels confident only during those times when he is in the spotlight, on the stage. To bolster himself, Chris kept hanging around the comedy clubs; he felt they were the only places that presented real comedy.

Chris objects when people lament that comedy is dying. Comedy is not dying, Chris feels; it is bad just because people like Billy Crystal, Eddie Murphy, and Whoopi Goldberg are not getting on the stage anymore. In recent comments about the state of comedy, Chris explains that he is doing an hour-and-20-minute show but that "comedy is so bad nowadays because comedians are geared to *The Tonight Show*, a five-minute set of jokes. Everything I talk about is a long topic. Even if you don't think its funny, you're not bored. 'He was wack, but he had a point about that AIDS stuff.'"

By the mid-1990s, Chris was not going anywhere that he wanted to be. He was 30 years old, and the only thing he knew how to do was stand-up comedy. He decided to give himself another year, and if he could not make it, he would give up the comedy business and get a "real" job.

6

ROLLING ON UP

❦

WHAT GOT CHRIS Rock rolling again was not just another break. It was the work ethic that his father has hammered into him when he was growing up. For Chris's family, the key to a satisfying life was hard work. As he pondered what his future would be, Chris realized that he had never looked at his chosen profession as work. It was fun. Now, without a real career in sight, he began to understand that comedy required the same dedication and drive as his father and mother had put into their jobs. Chris had talent, and he knew it. But he had not taken his comic skills seriously. To succeed, he had to hone and refine his work and prepare himself to get his career moving again. Chris began by studying the professionals, those he considered the best in the business. He began with his idol Sam Kinison and moved to Richard Pryor for stand-up delivery. He listened to all of Bill Cosby's albums and watched Eddie Murphy and George Carlin over and over again. To get a sense of their timing and presence onstage, he studied the routines of Don Rickles and Woody Allen.

When Chris felt he was ready, he took his new and improved material on the road, going back to the clubs where he could bring fresh routines to new audiences. He began to attract audiences that varied in race as well as in age, and he was moving into the mainstream of comedy. As he worked to hone his

"I know what pain is. 'Hi pain!' That's life." Chris titled his first HBO special Bring the Pain, *and it was an instant hit, making him one of the top young stand-up comics. Microphone in hand, he delivered blunt and gutsy reflections on everything from politics to race.*

material, he adjusted his routines to reflect changing events and added current observations about everything from women to politics to athletes to television to black rappers.

In 1996, it all paid off when he presented his HBO special *Bring the Pain,* which he wrote and coproduced. The hour-long show was taped at the Takoma Theater in Washington, D.C. He was nervous about how it would play, but he need not have been. His preacherlike oration, his politically incorrect comments, and his new-found sense of timing and delivery wowed the audience.

Pacing the stage with a devilish grin, he threw his barbs at women, black and white; world hunger; and "black people who hate niggas." He included a lacerating appraisal of the former black mayor of Washington, D.C., Marion Barry, whom he called "a crackhead." Critics were thrilled with the performance, hailing him as a racial and social commentator at the top of his form, assaulting the audience with his wit and insight even as they rocked with laughter. Chris Rock had walked onto the stage as a nearly out-of-work funny guy, and he strolled off as one of the hottest comics of the year.

Hamilton Cloud, executive producer of the NAACP's Image Awards, calls Chris a genius in his comedy. Cloud goes on to say how impressed he was with Chris when he first saw him perform in comedy clubs. Says Cloud, "I couldn't believe how politically insightful he was and how sharp he was during a time when black comedians weren't doing a lot of political stuff. The kid was up to speed on everything." And his friend Conan O'Brien declares, "He's a great stand-up. He seems so young, and he's a likable guy—that's probably why he can do really edgy stuff and get away with it."

Being up to speed meant winning an Emmy, television's highest honor, for the special. Chris was now ready to seize any and all opportunities to perform.

He made a few television commercials for Nike and appeared routinely on television shows, including a first appearance on *The Tonight Show*. On *Politically Incorrect*, Bill Maher's late-night program, he engaged in a routine with Maher about illegal immigration in California, in which Chris played the part of a roving political reporter. When Maher asked him what issues were upsetting people, Chris replied, "Well, one of the big things is illegal immigration. Everybody's talking about 'this is our land.' Hey, if it was our land, it wouldn't be called San Diego, OK? If it was really—you know, if it was really our land, it would be called Gus Johnson, all right?"

Chris's career was on a roll that seemed as though it would not stop. In 1997, he signed a deal with Dream-Works, Steven Spielberg's entertainment company, to make several comedy videos. That same year, he also inaugurated his *Chris Rock Show*, a late-night talkfest

Chris shows off his two Emmy Awards he received for his Bring the Pain *HBO special. At 31, he was definitely an established comedian and entertainer.*

on HBO. Now going into its fourth season, the show has gained an enthusiastic audience and has received critical acclaim. It is also irreverent and blunt. One observer noted that it is "so hard-hitting that the studio audience should be outfitted with air bags."

As a host, Chris has chatted with numerous celebrities, including the O. J. Simpson attorney Johnnie Cochran and two black leaders, Reverends Jesse Jackson and Al Sharpton. Jackson suggested Chris get involved in politics, an idea Chris dismissed with a shrug and the comment, "I'm in show business. I wanna hang out with Janet Jackson, not Jesse Jackson. Everybody wants you to talk to the kids. Kids don't wanna hear me talk—they wanna hear me tell *jokes*." Al Sharpton, who was Chris's favorite guest, said he would cut off his long hair if Chris would stop swearing. Chris declined.

Chris's involvement in his HBO show has not stopped him from other projects. His best-selling book *Rock This!*, a collection of his funniest jokes and an acerbic look at his life along with his opinions on almost everything, was published in 1997. He dedicated it to his father, "the funniest guy I've ever known." Chris also brought out a CD, *Roll with the New*, and renewed his stalled career in films. He was the voice of the guinea pig in Eddie Murphy's update of the film *Dr. Dolittle*, and he appeared with Mel Gibson and Danny Glover in the blockbuster hit *Lethal Weapon 4*.

The director of the film, Richard Donner, encouraged Chris to improvise and develop his character on the set. After the filming, Donner praised the young actor. "Chris Rock," he said, "is an extraordinary talent who never does or says anything the same way twice. His spontaneous creativity is a pleasure because it gives us so many options to work with." Critic Leonard Maltin chimed in with his review of *Lethal Weapon 4*: "Those wacky cops are at it again. . . . Added this time: Rock, as an

overzealous cop. . . . The cast is so likable and their energy so infectious that the filmmakers get away with murder."

Touring, writing, and promoting his CD kept Chris busy, prompting him to comment that he was the hardest-working comic in the business. His pal Conan O'Brien agrees. "Chris is someone who's done his homework. He's not trying to get by on style or attitude. He puts the work in." Some of Chris's work involves lending his presence to a variety of events, often by hosting award shows. In 1996, he took on the Billboard Awards in Las Vegas, and the following year he hosted the MTV Video Music Awards. To Chris's amazement, the show enjoyed the third-highest rating in the history of cable television. When his fans congratulated him, he replied with a joke: "You know how it is in music.

Chris welcomes famed O. J. Simpson attorney Johnnie Cochran to The Chris Rock Show. *Chris enjoys presenting controversial figures on his program. He once booked O. J. Simpson himself, but the network said no.*

Chris shares a scene from Lethal Weapon 4 *with Danny Glover (left) and Mel Gibson (right), the two wild cops of the series. It was Chris's first major film, and he was a hit as detective Lee Butters who is secretly married to Glover's daughter.*

Fickle. Here today, gone today." He also hosted the MTV Video Music Awards in September 1999.

No doubt his style contributed a great deal to the popularity of the 1997 MTV awards show. If confronted with a potentially unpleasant situation, Chris has a way of lightening it up. He had to present one of the awards to rapper Marion "Suge" Knight. Some rappers have an unfortunate habit of being involved in violent incidents. Chris is a nonviolent man, joking that his attitude stems from his thin, smallish build and the fact that in a fight, he would be beaten to a pulp. When he handed the award to Knight, who did not look too friendly or cheery, Chris smiled and quipped, "Don't kill me, Suge." Knight was not amused, and Chris quickly said "Suge, really, just kidding."

As well as hosting awards shows, Chris has been on the receiving end. In addition to his Emmys for *Bring the Pain*, he was given the Cable Ace Award for the best stand-up comedy special of 1995. Two years later, he received the Variety Special or Series Award for *The Chris Rock Show*. The same show earned him another Cable Ace Award for Entertainment Host. In 1999, he was honored with the NAACP's Image Award.

Chris's star was rising. With his reputation as a comedian, actor, and writer, the question was, would he go Hollywood? It does not seem likely. Although he loves moviemaking and has plans to make more, his heart is where it has always been— in stand-up comedy. He still lives in Brooklyn, and he still performs in the clubs. The audiences wait for his sharp one-liners, his sideways glances, the quick movements of his hands. This is Chris Rock in his element.

7

UP CLOSE AND PERSONAL

❧

Chris and his wife, Malaak Compton, share a rather conventional and unpretentious married life in a brownstone house on a quiet street in Brooklyn. When Chris is questioned about how Malaak views his routines that often put down women, he is cautious about answering and often dismisses the questioner.

WHEN YOUNG CHRIS began his comedy career, his father asked him if he was any good. Replied Chris, "I'm one of the best in the country." And as Julius Rock knew, his son did not lie. Chris's father and his family are never far from his mind or heart. His routines often include jokes about families. As he admits, "Families are a weird group of people," and he gladly reveals the presence of some oddballs in his own family. For Chris it is hard to imagine all these people getting together of their free will and saying, "Let's be a family." He chuckles, shakes his head, flashes that smile, and the audience laughs with him at the human silliness of it all.

Growing up with such strong family support and sharing so much with his siblings and the many foster children his mother cared for has given Chris a feeling for others. He strongly believes in family ties, and onstage he often integrates family situations into his routines. He has centered one routine around President Bill Clinton. Chris decided during one of his guest appearances on *SNL* that Clinton was an "honorary brother" because the president was going through such a troubled time. Chris was referring to the investigation surrounding the president's involvement with a young woman and the accusations against him of lying that ultimately led to Clinton's impeachment trial in 1999.

Chris agrees with the opinion of Tavis Smiley of Black Entertainment Television when Smiley commented on the impeachment proceedings against the president: "If Clinton thought he was an honorary brother before, he knows it for sure now. Black people feel for him. We know what it feels like to be dragged through the coals. You can never really know the pain of being black unless you are black, but Clinton is coming close."

Chris says the president just gets too much flack, and he muses that with Clinton in the White House, it's almost as if the nation actually does have a black president. According to Chris, that is because no one will leave him alone. The man, says Chris, has got "real problems," not just presidential problems.

Also in his routines, Chris often takes a dim view of the relationships between men and women, commenting generally that men can't be faithful and women can't be quiet. In talking about President Clinton's troubles, he put some of the blame on Hillary Rodham Clinton, characterizing her as a cold woman. He has talked about women and marriage with such comments as "Marriage is the roughest thing in the world," and "The whole idea of a woman is something that is regal and standoffish. You know, women wear makeup. They wear makeup and they wear heels. They're not themselves."

Despite these views, Chris is married; he and Malaak Compton were wed late in 1996. Malaak, a former public relations executive, had been his girlfriend for three years. A friend describes her as "really sweet, nice and hospitable, very warm." Chris credits his marriage with calming him down and his wife for giving him a center. But he generally does not like to talk about his marriage, and if questioned, says "Go on—move on." And he has refused to discuss his family with the comment, "They're not in show business."

Chris and Malaak have no pretensions and live a

relatively conventional life in a brownstone home in Brooklyn, not far from where he grew up, which they share with a dog named Essence Julius Rock. The "Essence" is for the *Essence* magazine awards show where the couple met, and of course the rest is for Chris's father. Rose Rock has commented that "I love the dog, but I still want a grandchild."

A persistent rumor has it that Chris chose to return to Bed Stuy, to his roots. He dismisses that idea with a laugh. "I'm not trying to keep it that real," he chuckles. And when Chris was asked, along with several other celebrities, what his first big purchase was with his newfound wealth, he admitted that he bought a $45,000 Corvette.

Chris is often seen at the Coffee Shop, an eatery

President Bill Clinton makes a statement about the impeachment proceedings. Chris believes that because President Clinton was going through such a troubled time that he could better understand what is was like to endure the difficulties of being an African American, and so Chris dubbed Clinton an "honorary brother."

on Manhattan's Union Square, where people give him some space. Sitting at his special table, without an entourage or security guards, he appears to be just another one of the guys. He dresses simply in what could be called off-the-rack clothes: jeans and a dark shirt over a T-shirt.

There are times, however, when he finds he cannot go where he wants to or do what he wants to do. He often finds himself surrounded by people—journalists, agents, managers, publicists. When Chris gets in an unhappy mood, he moans, "No one respects my space. Everybody wants something from me and they'll do anything to get it, regardless of my mood."

Comedian George Carlin knows what that is all about. He explains, "The public begins to see you as someone they know. They figure you're friendly 'cause you're always joking and stuff. I work well with that, because I'm a familiar face. Mine is a long-term relationship with the public. Chris still has that new-ness about him, which makes the public reaction a little more intense and harder for him to deal with."

When he is offstage, Chris sometimes seems ill at ease. In one instance he was attending a benefit concert in New York City at Radio City Music Hall. When he was asked to come up on the stage, he appeared uncomfortable and awkward. Several months later, confronted by reporters and flashing cameras at a Grammy party in New York City, he smiled stiffly and mumbled his words.

Chris's musings reflect the fact that in the entertainment world, security is precarious. The public is notoriously fickle, and executives and producers are as changeable and unpredictable as the weather. Contract or not, there is no guarantee that a television show will not be canceled or that the next special will be a hit or that the comedy gig will overwhelm the audience.

Chris is aware that he is a role model for young

people, especially young black Americans, and those who aspire to a career in comedy. With that in mind, in late 1999, he will start a humor magazine at Howard University. Howard is Malaak Rock's alma mater, a university begun following the Civil War as a place of higher learning for African Americans. Today it is open to all students, although its student body is still predominantly black. Howard University's library is the leading research institution on black history.

Chris has dubbed the magazine *Illtop*, after the university's newspaper, which is called *Hilltop*. In an interview, Robert Frelow of Howard University talked about the project: "Chris started it because he believes that there is a lack of black comedy writers in Hollywood. There are many black comics, but not

Chris plans to launch a humor magazine at Howard University, some of whose students are shown here at graduation. It will be called Illtop *in a spoof of the university's newspaper,* Hilltop.

writers. This project is part of an effort to train black writers in the art of comedy [which is] part of the School of Communications at Howard."

Chris has explained his reason for encouraging young black writers. "A lot of the [*Saturday Night Live*] writers came from Harvard, and I couldn't get anyone to help me write anything," he says. "I thought, if I ever got the chance, I'd start a black comedy magazine at a college."

Frelow explains Chris's thinking:

> Chris isn't saying that white people shouldn't write black comedy. That's fine with him. He's saying that blacks should have the same kind of training opportunity in college. *Illtop* will be kind of the black version of the *Harvard Lampoon*. And Chris is very involved in this. He spends time at Howard, runs seminars, and helps the students with comedy writing.

Since Chris writes his own material, he should be a very good teacher. His method of comedy writing is to first create a situation before writing jokes about it. He decides on a topic and then writes the jokes.

Chris also has other plans to keep him busy. He coproduces the television sitcom *The Hughleys* and is writing a script about a nerdy, skinny guy who actually gets the girl. He also says, "I want to direct, produce more shows, write another book—and I really want to be a good stand-up comic." He also is appearing in two new films, due out in 2000. *Nurse Betty* is a black comedy in which he and veteran actor Morgan Freeman costar with Renee Zellweger. In *Dogma*, a religious film, Chris plays an apostle of Jesus named Rufus who returns to earth and causes trouble. The film has caused some flack from religious groups. Chris shrugs it off with a joke, saying that when you depict Jesus as a black, it "doesn't make you popular."

Now in his 30s, Chris Rock thinks back on his

success, which, like that of most successful entertainers, did not happen overnight. He has worked
at his career, and he believes that part of his good
fortune in his chosen profession has come about
because he has matured. He was driven perhaps,
and he was certainly eager, but he was also naïve.
"I grew into this part," he says. The awkward years
are behind him. He enters into his comedy routines
thoroughly prepared.

Strange as it sounds, Chris credits a good deal of
his success to his unhappy, painful school years. He
explains that he might have had a happier and more
normal childhood in predominantly black schools,
but then he would probably have graduated into a
more conventional profession. He muses, "I wouldn't
think the way I do if I hadn't gone to a white school.
In a weird way, those people made me who I am."

8

IS THIS LANGUAGE REALLY NECESSARY?

❦

Sitting atop a cab on The Chris Rock Show, *Chris smiles impishly. His affable manner and boyish face belie the shouting, risk-taking young comedian whose use of foul language in many of his routines has brought criticism from several people, including some of his colleagues.*

FROM EARLY IN the 20th century until the late 1970s, acres of land in New York State's Catskill Mountains were dubbed the "Borscht Belt." The Jewish resorts that characterized the area gave it the name, after a popular soup served up to the clientele. Since entertainment, as well as food, was a mainstay of the resorts, the area was a haven for comics who called themselves the Borscht Belt comedians.

To make it in stand-up comedy, a comic had to make it in the Catskill resorts. The cast of comedians who got their start in the Borscht Belt is legion and includes Buddy Hackett, Myron Cohen, Sid Caesar, Danny Kaye, Jerry Lewis, Stubby Kaye, and countless others. Around the late 1970s, however, the Borscht Belt began fading as a popular resort area. And with its decline, it ceased to be the mecca for stand-up comedians. And like the change that overtook the area, the comedians who came later have changed too. Chris Rock would not have made it on the Borscht Belt. He is very much contemporary society's kind of comedian.

Chris is a black, stand-up funny man who takes a unique approach to serious issues that affect all of American society, white as well as black. There is hardly a contemporary subject that Chris will not hold forth on, dissecting it, very often commenting outrageously on what he sees as the pretensions and hypocrisy of modern society. Meeting touchy subjects head-on, he makes audiences laugh while he berates public figures or public activities he believes should change. It is difficult to imagine comedians of another generation, such as Danny Kaye or Sid Caesar, with the in-your-face style of Chris Rock.

Despite his popularity Chris does have critics. Many object to his language, which has been called dirty, offensive, degrading, and vulgar. Others also object to his racial material. Concerning the latter, Chris does not agree that it is so provocative. He claims other black comedians have done the same. "I don't talk about it any different than Richard [Pryor] did, or Dick Gregory," says Chris. "The wall I'm breaking down already has been broken down. Somebody just put wood paneling over it to cover the holes. It was much easier for me."

Nevertheless, his language is offensive to many who claim it is in bad taste and does not belong on the stage or on television. Although a fan of his, and a person Chris admires, Whoopi Goldberg has given him a slap on the wrist for what she considers overkill in his putdowns of celebrities. Because of his language his appearance on a segment of *Today*, an NBC early-morning show, was cut from a rebroadcast on the West Coast. In referring to Ken Starr, the independent counsel who investigated the scandals of the Clinton presidency, Chris had allowed as how he wanted to "whup" a certain part of Starr's anatomy. And, as noted, Bill Cosby still will not appear on Chris's show.

Chris might point out that he is not the only comic who uses profanity as part of a routine. Eddie Murphy, Martin Lawrence, and Joe Torry often curse and use foul language. Cosby and Sinbad, a well-known stand-up comedian, do not. Cosby has been an entertainer for more than 30 years without employing four-letter words. Sinbad says he once

Like Chris, comedian Martin Lawrence often offended people with his routines. Unlike Chris, however, Lawrence had a bad-boy reputation, which got him banned from the NBC network.

uttered a profanity on stage and has regretted it ever since. Another comedy star, Chris Tucker, thinks that today's crop of young comedians is too vulgar. Veteran Dick Gregory agrees, saying that many of the newcomers curse on stage because that's what Richard Pryor did. Young comics, says Gregory, "think they have to be vulgar to be funny. But they are doing themselves a disservice. Being funny and

Chris has appeared on many television talk shows, including the Oprah Winfrey Show. On her show he explained at length why he used some of the language he did in his routines.

being profane are two different things."

What does Chris say to all this? He firmly believes that fans see beyond his profanity and understand the messages in his comedy. Directing his scorn at those he feels deserve it does make his listeners and viewers sit up and take notice. They also take notice of his use of the n—— word and often object. Chris explained to Oprah Winfrey on her show why he used the word:

Our young people are using it to justify ignorance. So I pointed out that the people who use the word . . . people that are embracing the word are truly ignorant. . . . It's not a cool way to live. . . . It's like a lot of young black kids think it's cool to not know things, think it's cool to not follow the law, think it's cool to not behave themselves. That's not cool, that's ignorant. I just felt like pointing out the "nigorance" mentality. It has to stop."

There are times when Chris gets tired of having to explain using the n—— word. He feels he did explain why he uses the word in his first HBO special, describing the difference between black people and "niggas." "A black man that got two jobs, going to work every day, hates a nigga on welfare. 'Get a job! I got two: you can't get one?'"

Again, in an interview at his favorite restaurant, he protested about the assumptions some people have drawn from his comedy routines. "A whole lot of black people want to work," he said. "That's the only thing I hated about all the press I got in the last couple of years. . . . They act like I'm part of a minority of black folks that want to do the right things. No, I'm in the majority. I'm no freak of nature. I'm no different than that brother who's the busboy over there. You know?"

In our contemporary society, comedy has been able to lower the barriers of formerly taboo subjects partly through the advent of cable television, of which Comedy Central, a late-night cable network is an example. If *SNL* in its time was considered some-what shocking, for some Comedy Central really crosses the line. Any subject, issue, or person is fair game for laughter, whether in good taste or not and no matter what the language. The network does, however, stop short of pornography. Most Comedy Central viewers are between the ages of 18 and 49. The network is well aware of its audience and caters to it. Begun in 1991, the network is headed by a

56-year-old "true son of the '50s," Larry Divney. He says he grew up with the "last gasp of network radio" and he loves comedy. "I find people funny," he comments. "Humor helps get us through a lot."

Can the humor on Comedy Central or on Chris's HBO specials go too far? In 1998, Chris was presented on the television show *60 Minutes* with this introduction: "When a black comic takes on blacks and uses language no one would tolerate from a white comic and is very successful doing it in front of mixed audiences of blacks and whites, that's a story worth telling. Some black entertainers have walked all around it, but . . . no one has met it head-on quite like Chris Rock."

In the course of the interview, host Ed Bradley asked Chris about his HBO special of that year in which Chris verbally assaulted former Washington, D.C., mayor Marion Barry, who had been jailed for possession of crack cocaine. In response, Chris asked Bradley how it was possible to tell kids not to use drugs if the mayor was doing it. He pointed out that he was no harder on Barry than Jay Leno or David Letterman, who are television hosts, had been. Just because Barry is black, asked Chris, is he "supposed to think it's cool to smoke crack and be the mayor?" Concluded Bradley, "Rock says out loud what some people think but don't say."

On the same program, Chris's use of the n——word came up again. Explaining once more why he uses it, he said he loved blacks but did not see why he should like living next door to n——s. What is the difference between the two, he asked? Some black kids will do anything they can to get an education, take whatever jobs are available, endure the harshest of conditions to better themselves. And then, Chris continued, there are the others, those who sit back and figure out the easiest way to get money without working for it. Or those who sit back and try to take the money that you just worked for.

Those are the people Chris Rock does not want to have as neighbors.

Despite the criticisms, Chris is unafraid when it comes to facing just about anyone or any topic. When asked if his attacks on some people might be risky, he replies, "The risk is not being funny. Risky is being wack." He continues, "Fearless to me is like spitting on Mike Tyson—that's fearless. I mean, what I'm doing, I'm just trying to be funny."

Chris was not afraid to be critical when on one of his shows he took on the Reverend Jesse Jackson, who is one of Chris's political heroes. Hero or not, Jackson faced an unrelenting young comic. Although Chris claimed to be nervous about meeting Jackson, he lit into the civil rights activist, noting Jackson should be cleaning up the ghettos instead of making the polished, dramatic speeches for which he is known. While Jackson tried to explain the cutoff of federal funds for jobs, Chris kept right on talking, demanding to know why black kids cannot be encouraged to pick up a piece of trash in front of their own houses. "My mother used to make me clean up my yard and the two yards next door to us," he lectured a stuttering Jackson. He ended the interview by adding a few words about kids perhaps needing a "smack upside the head every now and then."

Chris further contends that comics ought to risk making fun of those close to them. He illustrated his point by talking about the deaths of two of his *SNL* friends, Chris Farley and Phil Hartman. Farley died from overdosing on drugs and alcohol. Hartman was shot and killed by his wife, who then shot herself. Making a grim joke, Chris observed that "Phil wanted to get out of the marriage. And he *did.* . . . Maybe his first instinct was right. She was psycho, that Brynn. He stayed because he was trying to help the people around him—kids, her, whatever." Chris has much the same ideas about the death of Farley, saying that he died for "pretty much the same reason—just

Although Chris admires the Reverend Jesse Jackson, he gave him a hard time when the civil rights activist appeared on his show. Usually not flustered, Jackson was not quite sure how to respond.

pleasing everybody." In continuing about the two entertainers and comedy in general, Chris bursts out: "Oh God, I have the same disease, the comedian curse. We're performers, a bunch of geeks no one liked. Now people really like us, and we're willing to . . . make ourselves miserable, to maintain it. Then, you know, we explode. Our wives shoot us, we OD [overdose] or whatever."

Chris has come under criticism for his attitude about O. J. Simpson and the so-called trial of the century. In fact, he wanted to have Simpson on his show, but the network owners objected, and Chris backed down. "When I was 24, I would have done it anyway," he says. "Who needs it? I worked too hard to get here." Chris did, however, make Simpson and the trial an issue during the taping of his *Bring the Pain* special. Chris was angry over the fact that so many whites criticized a nearly all-black jury for acquitting Simpson, claiming that if a white celebrity had been accused of such a murder, a white jury would have done the same. As he put it, "Because if that was Jerry Seinfeld charged with double murder and the only person that found the glove just happened to be in the Nation of Islam, Jerry'd be a free man."

Such sentiments do not always endear him to audiences, especially white audiences. But Chris also comes under attack from blacks. In 1997, he posed for a cover of *Rolling Stone* magazine with his neck grotesquely stretched upward. A computer-enhanced image depicted a hook jerking Chris off the stage. For some African Americans, the image of his stretched neck was too much of a reminder of the old days and the terrible lynchings of blacks. Chris was criticized again for appearing on the cover of *Vanity Fair* magazine as a clown with grease-painted lips. To many he looked like the stereotype of a clownish black in a vaudeville show.

Chris retorts to such criticisms by pointing out that he is a comedian. In a voice weary of trying to explain himself, he said, "You just want to try to be funny." And he concluded by saying he was fed up with the carping of some blacks, "especially so-called intellectuals," who don't know a joke when they see one.

Although it may seem as if nothing is sacred or will be spared from Chris's mocking, he does generally avoid some subjects. He doesn't say much about God, affirmative action, or the current state of leadership in the black community—aside from his swipes at former mayor Marion Barry and his confrontation with Jesse Jackson. About black leaders, he says, "I only know everybody who gets really big gets shot in the head. I'm sure that has deterred a few qualified brothers from stepping up to the mike." And he adds that "I'm not any more political than, you know, Peter Jennings [news anchor on ABC]. I'm just interpreting and putting a little comic spin on it."

Chris Rock is at the place he once dreamed of— the top. The *New York Times* has described him as "probably the funniest and smartest comedian working today." Despite the honors and accolades, he finds it hard to believe that at his young age he is in the precarious business of comedy. He wants to be known as a comic whose work will be remembered, like that of the elder comedians he so admires. Like every true performer, he wants and needs attention from those he entertains. That is why he works so hard.

Like any successful entertainer, Chris has learned that he cannot stay on top by standing still. In the first part of 1999, he toured the nation again, from California to Florida, using new and fresh routines to delight audiences. He also taped the ongoing *Chris Rock Show*, which begins its fourth season in the fall of 1999. Then in the summer of 1999, he taped a new HBO special, *Chris Rock: Bigger and Blacker*.

Taping the show at Harlem's Apollo Theater on three days in June, Chris delivered some brand-new routines which, when the show was aired on July 10, some critics reacted to with headlines such as "Rock rules, Rock rolls, Rock reels, Rock roars and sometimes, Rock riles." Chris does rile. One of his routines jabs at black women, and especially "fat black women" who, according to Chris, can be identified by the "fat over the pumps." Instead of black pride, he shouted, this was "fat pride." A woman who was in the audience at the Apollo took great exception to this assault. She is Star Jones, a woman of considerable size who is a former practicing attorney and cohost with five other women on the daytime talk show *The View*. The hosts discuss contemporary issues, especially those concerning women. On the next airing of *The View*, Jones took on Chris, criticizing him for his choice of material. True to form, however, Chris did not back down. "Fat pride" stayed in the routine.

When asked if Malaak, his wife, had seen the routine, Chris replied, "Yeah, she didn't say much." He has also admitted that marital problems helped shape some of his man-woman relationships in the show. Then, he noted that poking fun at marital problems helps give him a living, and a good one. "You know, that's how we eat," he said.

Chris Rock: Bigger and Blacker shows the comedian at his best. He comes on stage at full throttle, running and talking, a slender body dressed in a silver suit that looks made from space material. He wears small gold earrings that frame a boyish, almost endearing face. He looks impish and likable. From the moment he speaks, he has the audience in his grip. Most of the audience, but not all, are African Americans. Whoever they are, they love him.

Right from the start, it is obvious that this comedian is different from most stand-up comics. He does not stand still with the microphone gripped firmly in one hand. He moves. Chris assaults the stage. He darts from left to right, from right to left, in long, swift strides. He shifts the mike from hand to hand while talking incessantly. Smiling, mugging, Chris stares out at the crowd and, directing his shafts at society, challenges the audience with questions such as "Whatever happened to crazy?" and then tells them. "The world is real crazy. You know why? 'Cause I'm more scared of *white* kids than black kids." Referring to the Columbine High School massacre that occurred earlier in the year in Littleton, Colorado, he demands that the audience listen. "Damn trench coat Mafia," he shouts. "When I was a kid . . . we separated the crazy kids from everybody

By 1999, Chris Rock had reached the top of his profession. That same year, the young stand-up comedian who had made his way up from the ghetto received one of the highest awards given by Essence magazine— that of outstanding African American.

else. They got out of school at 2:30 P.M., not 3 o'clock, just in case they wanted to kill somebody."

Nothing escapes Chris's scrutiny—from school violence to single-parent families to presidential scandals to taxes and social security to racism. "We [blacks] don't hate Jews. We hate all white people." Or, blacks "should get Social Security at 29" because they don't live much beyond 65. Scarcely a moment passes when Chris is not talking. How can he possibly remember all this material?

Through this nonstop, hour-long monologue, two things stand out. He peppers his talk with raunchy language and four-letter words, smothering his audience with them. He repeats them again and again, as though making certain everyone has heard him. Then, suddenly there are periods, perhaps two or three minutes long, when he rails against society and its ills without making one off-color comment or four-letter exclamation. The audience responds just as enthusiastically and laughs just as heartily.

The second thing that is prominent in Chris's material is that behind all the language and insults Chris Rock is delivering a message. It may seem strange coming from this hip, cool guy with the smart mouth because it is an old-fashioned theme. Behind all the jive, he is talking about traditional morality, a work ethic, and being responsible for what you do. These values may not be so strange after all. They are those he learned from his mother and father back in Bed Stuy.

Fans love him and his material, and critics have taken to him. *Chris Rock: Bigger and Blacker*, however, was not received quite as well by critics as *Bring the Pain*. Said one, "If you compare this new hour-long virtuoso recital to Rock's last HBO special . . . *Bigger and Blacker* suffers slightly, but it would be more fair to compare it with what all other comedians are doing these days and then there's no contest." The critic continues, "Rock's delivery seemed more craftily modulated in *Bring the Pain*, and sometimes in *Bigger and Blacker*, he becomes strident and shrill. But then he'll zing you with an insight so fresh and sassy that the content justifies the style." The writer concludes, however, that Chris is "on a rarefied, roarified plane, and his material remains bolder and more meaningful than that of almost any mainstream comic one can think of."

Chris Rock has paid his dues, and it has put him where he wants to be at this point in his life. His goals of more stand-up comedy, writing, probably directing, and turning out CDs and films can be all wrapped up in his own appraisal of himself: "I want to be great. That's my drive. Plain and simple."

CHRONOLOGY

1966   Born Chris Rock on February 7 in Andrews, South Carolina, to Rose and
        Julius Rock

1972   Moves to Bedford Stuyvesant section of Brooklyn, New York

1983   Drops out of all-white high school; takes odd jobs in restaurants; begins
        performing in evenings at comedy clubs around New York

1986   Spotted by comedian and actor Eddie Murphy at the Comic Strip

1987   Signed by Eddie Murphy for HBO show *Uptown Comedy Express*; makes film
        debut as parking attendant in film *Beverly Hills Cop 2*

1990   Joins cast of television comedy show *Saturday Night Live*

1991   Plays crack addict in film *New Jack City*

1992   Promoted to regular player on *Saturday Night Live*

1993   Leaves *Saturday Night Live*; joins cast of short-lived variety series *In Living
        Color*; cowrites, produces, and stars in film *CB4*

1994   Headlines HBO *Chris Rock Comedy Special*

1995   Receives Cable Ace Award for Best Stand-Up Comedy Special of the Year

1996   Makes first appearance on *Tonight Show*; begins making television commercials;
        writes, coproduces, and performs HBO special *Bring the Pain*; marries
        Malaak Compton

1997   Is executive producer and star of HBO talk show *The Chris Rock Show*; hosts
        MTV Video Music Awards; publishes book *Rock This!*; receives two Emmy
        Awards for Music and Comedy Special for *Bring the Pain*

1998   Plays feature role in *Lethal Weapon 4*

1999   Tours country; presents HBO special *Chris Rock: Bigger and Blacker*; receives
        NAACP's Image Award; hosts MTV Video Music Awards; funds black
        college humor magazine, *Illtop*

TELEVISION APPEARANCES

Cable Television

Uptown Comedy Express (HBO, 1987)

Chris Rock Comedy Special (HBO, 1994)

Bring the Pain (HBO, writer and executive coproducer, 1996)

The Chris Rock Show (HBO, executive coproducer and star, 1997)

Video Music Awards (MTV, host, 1997)

Chris Rock: Bigger and Blacker (HBO, writer and executive coproducer, 1999)

Video Music Awards (MTV, host, 1999)

Network Television

Saturday Night Live (cast member, 1990–93)

In Living Color (cast member, 1993)

Tonight Show (guest, 1996)

Politically Incorrect (guest, 1996)

Saturday Night Live (guest, 1999)

FILMOGRAPHY

———— ❧ ————

Beverly Hills Cop 2 (1987)

I'm Gonna Git You Sucka (1990)

New Jack City (1991)

CB4 (cowriter, producer, and star, 1993)

Dr. Dolittle (voice, 1997)

Lethal Weapon 4 (featured role, 1998)

Dogma (1999)

Nurse Betty (2000)

AWARDS

Cable Ace Award for Best Stand-Up Comedy Special of the Year (1995)

Emmy Award for Writing Outstanding Variety, Music or Comedy Special (1996)

Cable Ace Award for Entertainment Host (1997)

Emmy Award for Comedy Special for *Bring the Pain* (1997)

Emmy Award for Music for *Bring the Pain* (1997)

Variety Special or Series Award for *The Chris Rock Show* (1997)

Essence Magazine Award as Outstanding African American (1999)

NAACP Image Award (1999)

BIBLIOGRAPHY

"Are Young Black Comedians Talking Too Dirty?" *Jet,* January 1998.

Baldwin, Kristen. "The Hot Rock." *News Notes*, 19 September 1997.

Blue, Rose. *Bed Stuy Beat.* New York: Franklin Watts, 1980.

Buchalter, Gail. "I'd Rather Tell the Truth." *The Phildelphia Inquirer*, 29 August 1999.

Cader, Michael. *Saturday Night Live: The First 20 Years*. Boston: Houghton-Mifflin, 1994.

Chappell, Kevin. "Chris Rock." *Ebony*, May 1997.

"Chris Rock: Comedian and Actor." *Newsmakers*, 14 March 1999.

"Chris Rock." *Contemporary Black Biography*. Detroit: Gale, 1998.

"Chris Rock: A Rock Solid Comic." *EM*, April 1997.

Ebert, Roger. "Lethal Weapon 4." *Chicago Sun-Times*, 24 June 1999.

Farley, Christopher John. "Seriously Funny." *Time*, 13 September 1998.

Fretts, Bruce. "Chris Rock." *The Entertainers*, 26 December 1997.

Rock, Chris and David Rensin. *Rock This!* New York: Hyperion, 1997.

"Rock on a Roll." *Essence*, November 1998.

60 Minutes, Burrelle's Transcripts, 6 September 1998.

Tannenbaum, Rob. "Stand-Up Guy." *TV Guide*, 10–16 July 1999.

Tucker, Ken. "Rocking Late Night." *Television*, 28 November 1997.

Watson, Margeaux. "For Those About to Rock . . ." *Time Out New York*, 8–15 July 1999.

INDEX

PICTURE CREDITS

page

2: The Everett Collection
3: The Everett Collection
10: The Everett Collection
13: The Everett Collection
16: AP/Wide World Photos
19: Ron Wolfson/London
    Features Int'l
20: Nick Elgar/London
    Features Int'l
24: AP/Wide World Photos
27: AP/Wide World Photos
28: AP/Wide World Photos
31: AP/Wide World Photos
33: Ed Weidman/London
    Features Int'l
35: Judge Richard Salzman

38: The Everett Collection
40: The Everett Collection
44: The Everett Collection
49: The Everett Collection
51: AP/Wide World Photos
52: Khu Bui/AP/Wide
    World Photos
54: Photofest
56: The Everett Collection
59: AP/Wide World Photos
61: The Everett Collection
62: The Everett Collection
64: The Everett Collection
67: Kevork Djansezian/AP/
    Wide World Photos
69: The Everett Collection

70: Photofest
72: Ron Wolfson/London
    Features Int'l
75: J. Scott Applewhite/AP/
    Wide World Photos
77: Khue Bui/AP/Wide
    World Photos
80: The Everett Collection
83: The Everett Collection
84: Steve Green/AP/Wide
    World Photos
88: Mary Ann Chastain/AP/
    Wide World Photos
92: Stuart Ramson/AP/
    Wide World Photos

ROSE BLUE, an author and educator, has written more than 50 books, both fiction and nonfiction, for young readers. Her books have appeared as TV specials and have won many awards. A native New Yorker, she lives in the borough of Brooklyn.

CORINNE J. NADEN, a former U.S. Navy journalist and children's book editor, also has more than 50 books to her credit. A freelance writer, she lives in Tarrytown, New York, where she shares living quarters with her two cats, Tigger and Tally Ho!

NATHAN IRVIN HUGGINS, one of America's leading scholars in the field of black studies, helped select the titles for the BLACK AMERICANS OF ACHIEVEMENT series, for which he also served as senior consulting editor. He was the W. E. B. DuBois Professor of History and Afro-American Studies at Harvard University and the director of the W. E. B. DuBois Institute for Afro-American Research at Harvard. He received his doctorate from Harvard in 1962 and returned there as professor in 1980 after teaching at Columbia University, the University of Massachusetts, Lake Forest College, and the California State University, Long Beach. He was the author of four books and dozens of articles, including *Black Odyssey: The Afro-American Ordeal in Slavery*, *The Harlem Renaissance*, and *Slave and Citizen: The Life of Frederick Douglass*, and was associated with the Children's Television Workshop, National Public Radio, the Boston Athenaeum, the Museum of Afro-American History, the Howard Thurman Educational Trust, and Upward Bound. Professor Huggins died in 1989, at the age of 62, in Cambridge, Massachusetts.